ELSEWHERE

A Long Lakes Thriller

Antonella L.M. Rivalta

A page-turning romantic suspense novel that will keep you on the edge of your seat.

An ocean away from her friends and family in Milan, Valentina Bianco wants nothing more than to leave the drama of her disastrous first marriage behind, while carrying on her wine importing business in idyllic Long Lakes, Tennessee . . . in a log cabin she calls *Elsewhere*. She's been hurt before, so romance is the last thing on her mind.

Enter Jack Erikson. Her newest neighbor may be handsome, and nothing can stop the powerful attraction they share. But he is also a mysterious outsider . . . with a secret that will send shockwaves rippling through the small town.

No, Long Lakes is not the quiet, bucolic refuge from danger that it appears to be. Not by a long shot. Hidden behind the community's gates is a web of lies and deceit . . . perhaps even murder.

And when Jack begins to scratch around, falling deeper and deeper to the community's dark underbelly . . . neither of them are safe, and only one thing is for certain . . . Life in *Elsewhere* will never be the same.

Contents

"When you harbor bitterness, happiness will dock elsewhere." – Andy Rooney

Prologue

Annie Harvey couldn't have wished for a better gift for her twentieth anniversary.

It was a gorgeous early spring morning, with a sun-dappled canvas of bright green spring leaves overhead. Cool—but not cold—air braced her skin, and the sounds of birds chirping and insects buzzing their spring welcome was like a love song made exclusively for her and her beloved.

Her dear husband.

Though the Great Smoky Mountains might have been the most visited National Park in all of the country, right now, it was just the two of them, forging their own trail for an early-morning hike to catch breakfast at the summit. A perfect way to cap off their romantic weekend getaway.

Sure, people had been lost for days and weeks stepping off the beaten path, but War? He'd practically grown up on these mountains. And that was what she loved about him—he had an adventurous spirit, and where she preferred to stick to the well-known, he *always* took the way less travelled. For two decades, he'd drawn her out of her comfort zone, made life interesting.

Sometimes a little *too* interesting, but that's what marriage was about. Taking the good with the bad.

As she stepped over another exposed route in the earth, she looked up at her husband of twenty years. He slashed through the brush like a hardy explorer of old, eager to claim the summit of Balsam High Top. Strong and slim, he'd stayed in shape over the decades with daily runs. Now, at nearly fifty, he was still as handsome as ever in his cargo pants and flannel shirt. He easily could've passed for someone fifteen years younger.

A flush of pride crept from her cheeks, down her neck. He wasn't romantic by nature. No, more than that, he lived to surprise her, to throw her off her game. This whole weekend had been his suggestion—the quaint bed and breakfast, the candlelit restaurant nestled in the mountains, the strawberries and champagne that had been delivered to their room, which they'd fed to each other late at night, in bed. All of it . . . perfect.

After everything they'd been through, it nearly brought tears to her eyes.

She'd finally gotten the man she married back.

The terrain was rough, and they'd been climbing for an hour. Every so often, he'd turn, ask her, "You okay, kid?", just like he had nearly a quarter of a century ago, when they were high school sweethearts. She was far from a kid, though, now. Back then, he'd been a little gangly, maybe, but still good-looking. He'd been oh-so-attentive to her every whim, charming even her shotgun-toting, never-impressed pastor daddy into eagerly agreeing to the sacrifice of his only daughter's hand in marriage.

He'd impressed everyone. Even she'd been impressed, when that gangly kid went on to become a banker in Cookeville, member of the Board of Trustees, HOA president, and a respected member of the community. They'd had two children, now grown. A beautiful home in Eastern Tennessee. Yearly family vacations. A good life together, making them the envy of their neighbors.

Then came the rough patch.

The other woman. She cringed at the thought. In one horrible evening, she'd gone from thinking she was the envy of suburban housewives everywhere to a massive joke whose entire life was a lie.

But that was over, now.

All marriages had their difficulties. She'd been worried, of course. Who wouldn't be? He'd had a mid-life crisis, headed off on the wrong path, made questionable decisions. It happened to the best of men.

All he had needed was a little guidance from a good woman to lead him back.

And Annie had done that. It wasn't easy. Caught in the clutches of that other woman, dragged down by the devil, he'd insisted upon a divorce.

She'd told him she'd sooner die than see the marriage she had put two decades into come to an end.

Then one night, two months ago, he'd come to her with tears in his eyes. Actual tears. She hadn't seen him cry, ever. He apologized, told her that he'd been wrong. That he couldn't live life without her. She'd insisted on marriage counseling, set down ground rules, told him that things would have to change, big-time. The women? Gone. The shady side-business? Done.

He agreed.

Now, everything was right. The worst was over.

At a particularly steep part of the path, her husband broke into a jog to climb over several small boulders.

Annie fanned her face. If only she'd been as religious about her own exercise routine as she'd been about attending Sunday mass. She hadn't exactly let herself go, but she definitely wasn't twenty anymore. "War. Not so fast," she huffed.

He stopped, looked back at her with a charming little smirk, swinging the picnic basket to his other hand. "Come on, kid. Almost there."

She hustled to keep up. As she reached him, he extended his free hand to her. She took it, her heart fluttering as their eyes locked.

"It's so beautiful here!" she gushed, breathless, more from her husband's intense gaze than from the exertion. Their lovemaking last night, after nearly six months of sleeping in separate beds, had been *so* good. Easily the best night of her life. She'd lapped him up like an oasis in the desert, greedily, thirstily. Her entire body tingled at the thought.

He hoisted her up, and her hiking boots slipped against the damp rocks before she found solid footing. There were a lot of old leaves on the ground, wet from recent rain, which could be slippery, but she didn't worry.

Not with her husband there. Her protector.

He locked onto her wrist firmly, ensuring she wouldn't slip. "Watch it, now."

She let out a girlish giggle. "Oh. Thanks."

Now that they were at the top of the hill, the tree-cover gave way to a cloudless sky and massive white rocks, baking in the heat. Her pale skin stung from the unforgiving sun. She shielded her eyes and peered out over the lush green canopy of trees below them. In the distance, blue mountains rose up against the horizon, distant shadows against a pale blue sky.

In seconds, he was ahead of her again. She swiped a hand over her damp forehead, then unzipped and shrugged off her jacket, wrapping it around her waist. "There yet?"

"Not much longer."

Ten minutes later, they arrived. The outpost was a flat area with a gorgeous 360 view of nothing but nature's green majesty, stretching on for miles and miles. No picnic benches, no signs of human life at all. Setting down the picnic basket, he stretched his arms over his head. "This'll do. What do you think?"

She looked around. He said this would be the best vista in the park, and of course, he was right. "Amazing!"

She perched upon a rock, taking in deep breaths of mountain air as she scanned the area below. As she was bending over to reach for the picnic basket, she heard it.

A decidedly human cry.

She tilted her chin up and spied Warren. He was still, too. Listening. He'd heard it, as well.

"What was that? A wild animal?"

"Probably. Nothing to worry about." He shrugged and peered through the brush. "You set up the picnic. I'll check it out."

Before she could tell him to be careful, he disappeared through the trees.

She reached into the basket and pulled out the blanket, which she spread out on the rock. She paused to listen, but it didn't come again. It could have been a child, shrieking in glee.

Or a person, screaming in agony.

Wind whistled through the trees, and the sweat on her skin felt cold suddenly. She thought she heard footsteps, but when she looked around, no one was near. "Warren?" she called.

No answer.

Straightening, she headed in the direction of the noise, into the woods.

The skeletal branches of smaller brush clawed at her the LL Bean jacket around her waist as she took another few steps into the woods, toward the ledge. She crunched over a blanket of old leaves, pushing aside branches that threatened to poke her eyes.

All at once she came to a rocky ledge she hadn't expected. Teetering on the edge, she looked over, but saw nothing but some scrubby pine trees.

She sighed and was about to turn back when something glinted in the periphery of her vision.

She paused, squinting at it. It was nothing obvious, but still, something that didn't quite fit in. She craned her neck, unable to make it out.

Whatever the sound was, it hadn't come from there. That was too far away. The sound was probably just an animal. Noises echoed around these mountains, making it impossible to tell which came from where.

She pushed her glasses up on her nose and looked closer. Her eyes certainly weren't what they once were. And did it even matter? Her husband, everything that mattered in her life, was over *here*, on this peak.

Suddenly, a branch cracked underfoot. She spun.

But there was nothing behind her but the trees. "War? Is that you?"

Again, no answer. Shaking her head, she turned her attention toward the view and sucked in a deep, bracing breath.

It was the last breath she'd ever take. A moment later, she felt a strong, solid push on her back, and then she went airborne, face first into the gully. She didn't have time to fight, but she had time to scream.

Unfortunately, no one heard.

At least, no one who cared.

Chapter One

Nothing ruined a beautiful spring morning more than *him*.

Valentina Bianco tore her gaze from the magnificent greenery and lush surroundings of the forest, adjusted her position on the saddle, and fished the buzzing phone out of her pocket. She sighed when Antonio's picture appeared on the display. *What does he want?*

She pocketed the phone. He could wait.

Bitterness crowded her thoughts. *Forever*.

Then she thought of her nineteen-year-old daughter, Beatrice, in her dorm in Nashville, packing and nervously chewing her fingernails to the quick at the thought of her first solo trip to Italy.

Valentina frowned.

Okay. *Not* forever.

Just a little longer.

To think, Valentina used to enjoy weddings. Romance. Love. Now, she broke into hives whenever anyone even mentioned it.

That was for other people. Not her.

Patting Sunny's side, she snapped the reins and broke into a gallop toward the barn, trying not to think of her ex-husband. Of course, that never worked. She'd been thinking about him more and more, the closer his wedding date got.

When she arrived at the barn, Molly was waiting for her, flashing a big, toothless smile. The poor woman wasn't thirty yet, and yet she looked older—skeletal body, pitted skin, rotted teeth. She'd have been pretty, if it wasn't for her obvious battle against the addiction demons. Meth, possibly. Molly was good with horses, though, and that was all that Valentina cared about.

"*Grazie,* Molly," she said, handing her Sunny's reins.

"No problem. Nice ride?" Molly asked.

Phone already in hand, Valentina murmured a yes and stared at the dark display like it was the plague. As she meandered toward her car, she took deep breaths, trying to mentally prepare herself. Then she dialed the phone and lifted it to her ear.

He answered right away. "Valentina."

He always used the same tone with her now, like she was a naughty schoolgirl who needed to be corrected, and not the wife she'd been to him for over twenty years.

"Antonio," she responded in kind, the word clipped.

"I just got off the phone with Beatrice," he said in Italian to her as she climbed into her red Ford 150 pickup, the first major purchase they'd made when they relocated to the States, three years ago. "She tells me she's nervous."

No small talk. No "How are you, how's the weather there?" That suited her fine. The quicker this conversation went, the better.

"She has to learn to travel on her own someday. She's nineteen," Valentina said as she pulled down the visor and stared at herself in the mirror. She may have been coming up on forty-six years old, but she still looked good, not a gray hair or wrinkle in sight. Unlike the tramp she'd been left for. What Antonio saw in that woman, Valentina would never understand. Funny, she'd spent all of her life trying to stay in shape and look good for the man she married, and he'd up and fallen for Manuela, an awkward, mousy researcher from his office.

The first of many things she'd never understand about men.

The whole lot of them was hopeless. It was better just to stay away.

Antonio went on, rambling in his worry, finishing with, "I don't know if she'll get on the plane."

Valentina rolled her eyes. Poor Beatrice had inherited his tendency to obsess about practically everything. "She'll get on the plane. Once she's in the air, she'll be fine."

"I suppose you know best."

She pushed up the visor and sighed. "Is that all?"

"No . . . why, Valentina," his voice lilted, oozing the same charm she'd fallen for a lifetime ago. "If I didn't know better, I'd think you were eager to get off the phone with me. Do you have plans?"

She scowled. He was teasing her, now. Though she'd have loved to keep him guessing about the mysterious, exciting life she'd been living since the divorce, she got the feeling he knew better than anyone that she'd quietly thrown herself into her work. Work . . . and nothing else. "Yes, I do. I must go."

Without giving him a chance to respond, she ended the call. She threw the phone onto the passenger seat, tossed her head back, and opened her mouth in a silent scream.

14

Then she started the engine and headed out of the lot.

The gated community where she lived had it all. Or at least, it used to, until it had gone bankrupt. She found herself cursing every pothole in the gravel road as she bumped along past the general store. Remembering last-minute that she was low on olive oil for tonight's dinner, she hung a quick left and pulled into the parking lot.

As usual, the lot was empty.

Well, except for a sleek black BMW. Valentina knew most of the cars that belonged to her neighbors. The BMW wasn't one of them.

Gnashing her teeth, she marched up the stairs and pulled open the door to the log-frame building. She spotted the offender right away.

A stranger, standing at the check-out, back to her. Chatting with Ellie, of course. Ellie could carry on a conversation with a wall.

A *stranger*, who didn't belong here in their gated community. Using the facilities deemed *only* for residents. Of course, Ellie was being too soft to give him directions to the Piggly Wiggly and send him on his way.

Valentina charged ahead, fists clenched, just as Ellie let out a high-pitched, eardrum-grating giggle.

"You shouldn't be here!" she snapped as he bent over a paper bag, placing a bag of tortilla chips on the very top of it. "This is for —"

She stopped dead in her tracks and lost her voice when the man turned and locked eyes with her.

It was like fate was mocking her. Just when she'd decided to swear off men for good, someone had dropped the best looking one she'd ever seen, right in front of her.

Dio santo, Valentina. You'd think you've never seen a man before.

Chapter Two

Jack Erikson could do nothing but smirk dumbly as the raven-haired spitfire of a lady tore into him.

And here, he'd just begun to think all the people in this neck of the Tennessee woods were so hospitable.

Now, as he finished packing the bread—all they had was white Wonder Bread, which made him feel like he was five again—into his shopping bag, he took a deep breath, trying to calmly gauge the situation, just as he'd been taught at Quantico.

The last thing he needed was to call attention to himself.

Unfortunately, this woman seemed to have the opposite desire. She rattled on like gunfire, accusing him. Of what, he wasn't quite sure, because half of what she said was in another language. Italian, he guessed. What was an Italian lady doing way out here in the sticks?

When she paused to take a much-needed breath, he held up his hands in surrender. "I'm sorry. Did I do something wrong?"

"Did you do something wrong?" she parroted, looking up at the ceiling, maybe for God, to give her strength. "Have you not even been listening to anything I said?"

He had been. Something about trespassing. About how he shouldn't be here. After that, he'd gotten lost.

At any other time, he would've reached into his pocket and flashed his credentials. His admission ticket to pretty much anywhere.

But he'd left those at home, as he usually did for undercover work. He'd also left behind his gun, his suit, his equipment—anything that would've made him stick out, since federal agents had a way of doing that, arousing suspicion. Luckily for him, he was the kind of guy people liked. He didn't make enemies. Strangers talked to him. He must've had a kind, pleasant face that drew people in.

Too bad he hadn't figured on this woman being here.

Maybe he should've known. It was just the kind of luck he'd been having lately with the opposite sex. *Bad* luck.

"Yeah." He rubbed the back of his neck and pointed to his groceries. Mostly junk, since it was possible the concept of health hadn't yet reached this far into the rural center of Tennessee. "I'm sorry. I was just getting—"

She crossed her arms. "The general store is only for residents."

"Ah. Well, I'm renting an apartment on the premises," he said. He'd hoped to defuse the situation, but before he could get the last word out, her eyes filled with fire.

Shit. He'd said something wrong. *Again.*

"Is that so? From whom?"

He wasn't used to taking orders, but something about this woman's manner harkened back to his drill sergeant in basic training. He scrambled to grab a slip of paper from the pocket of his jeans.

He'd written the guy's name and phone number hastily before he left, in case he should run into maintenance issues. Unfolding it, he said, "Tom Matthews?"

She threw up her hands and unleashed a string of Italian—probably curses—into the air. "That's just fine," she muttered, like it was anything but. "I'm going to have a talk with *Tom*."

Jack gritted his teeth. He'd taken an oath to protect the American people, not to put innocent ones on someone's shit list.

He peered over at the lady behind the register, a cherubic blonde woman with a welcoming smile that had earlier made him dare to think this whole ordeal would be rainbows and sunshine. The blonde had a vest stretching over her large breasts, the chest pocket embroidered with the name *Ellie* in neat script.

Ellie shook her head, an amused smile stretched from apple cheek to apple cheek, and whispered conspiratorially, "Renters aren't *technically* allowed at Long Lakes."

"Ah."

So the Italian Lady was one of those. The community sticklers. The nosy ones who prowled the streets, got up in everyone's business, and ensured all the rules in the development were followed to a tee.

And now he was on her bad side.

Not good.

His assailant stared at him, arms crossed, fingers tapping, waiting for some sort of reply. Did she expect him to admit he was wrong and go back to where he came from? Probably.

He couldn't do that. There were few things in his life that mattered much anymore, but his job was at the top of that list, in space number three, right under his kids, Lily and Brayden.

He started in again, his voice low and calm. "Well, I didn't know that, and I paid Tom for the m—"

"Then I'll talk to Warren, our HOA president," she said, gesturing wildly with her hands, no calmer than when she'd first spun in here like a massive tornado.

If anything, she was just getting worse, a fact made even more obvious when Ellie rolled her eyes and said, "Easy, Val. You're not being nice to our guest."

The woman swung her wrath toward Ellie. "He's not a guest. He's an intruder. The next thing you know, he'll want to use our pool. Our facilities. And I know I'm not the only one in this development who's sick of working day and night to keep this place nice just for any old person to use it." When Ellie didn't have a reply, she added, "And for the last time, *El*. It's *Valentina*."

Tenacious. She clearly wasn't going to let this go. Her dark hair was windblown, and she wore jeans and a fleece pullover, with a little bit of mud on her boots, suggesting she'd just come in from some kind of exercise. Definitely in shape, despite being early forties. She'd be pretty—gorgeous, even—if she weren't so hell-bent on tearing him a new one.

He let out a breath. "All right. I'm sorry. Do what you've got to do." He lifted the groceries into his arms. "But I've got a book to write."

That was the story, anyway.

Before he could make a move toward the door, Valentina let out a huff of air, turned on her heel, and marched to the door, throwing it open and stalking through.

Jack watched through the window as she climbed into a massive pick-up truck, as fiery as its owner's temper. "Nice woman."

Ellie laughed and handed him his receipt. "I hope you don't let the one bad apple spoil the bunch. We're all very friendly here. I promise."

He flashed her his charming smile, and instantly regretted it when her eyes drifted to his ring finger. Though the divorce had been final for months, he hadn't brought himself to remove the plain gold band.

It didn't matter. He never had trouble attracting women with that two-dimpled smile of his, and the ring seemed to reel them in, even faster. Especially the women with husbands of their own.

He knew the dance. After checking for the ring, she'd casually mention where they might run into each other again.

But he didn't play that game. Hell, no.

"Let me ask you a question. Seeing as how renting's not too popular with the residents . . . Who does one talk to around here if they're interested in buying?"

Her eyes lit up. "You want to *stay* here?"

Not on your life. He shrugged. "If I like it."

She batted her eyelashes. "That would be *lovely*. But I don't know who you'd ask. My husband handled all that business stuff. I'm just his trophy wife."

He smiled obligingly. "Fortunate for you."

"So what kind of book are you writing?" she asked him as he rolled up the receipt and tucked it in his wallet. "Is it your life story?"

"A fantasy novel." He'd practiced this answer a hundred times on the two-and-a-half-hour drive from Nashville. All he'd done since the divorce was think about his cases. The other agents called him a machine, for how laser-focused he was on closing them out. He was on track for Agent of the Year.

This one was routine. Open and shut bankruptcy fraud. Once he collected enough evidence, he'd be in and out of here in a few days.

"Oh, you mean like . . ." Ellie's face was a mask of sheer confusion. Clearly not a Tolkien fan.

He decided to help her out. "Yeah. Like you know, orcs and trolls and things. Middle Earth. Legendary battle between good and evil."

She smiled, but not before a look of disgust crossed her face. "Oh. Nice," she said tightly. "Can't say I read much of that. Or really . . . anything, anymore. Too busy. I used to read, like, romance, in high school. Have you ever read *Flowers in the Attic?*"

He shook his head. "Is it good?"

"Amazing. You really should. Well, I hope I'll see you around! If you need anything, I'm the first cabin you come to on the right, right down this road. If you just go out this way . . ."

She pointed meaningfully in a number of directions, but he nodded along, uninterested.

He had other things on his mind than the game she was playing.

No, the game he was interested in was finding out what the shady developer of Long Lakes was up to, and getting the hell out of this middle-of-nowhere, backwoods town.

When he stepped outside into the late morning sunshine, he was surprised to see the red truck, idling beside his own. Its occupant, dwarfed by the steering wheel, stared down at something in her lap, probably her phone, so all he could make out was a mass of wild, dark curls.

He had to go near it because his BMW was parked beside it. As he did, a strong urge overtook him. Before he could think better of it, he rapped on the passenger-side window.

The second she looked up, her eyes narrowed, and he almost wished he hadn't. But he was a peacemaker. It was the reason he'd tried to make things work with Yvonne, long after they'd been broken beyond repair. And even if he wasn't in town long, it didn't hurt to be nice to the locals. Especially the nosy ones. There was no telling what kind of information a woman like her could provide.

She powered the window down and raised an eyebrow, as if asking, *What do you want?*

"Just wanted to clear the air. You see, I'm also thinking of buying in this area. It's really beautiful," he said, flashing that charming smile of his. The smile that worked. The smile that leveled rooms of women. "Think you might be interested in giving me a tour?"

To his surprise, she scowled at him. "Ask Ellie for a tour. I'm sure she'll be more than willing," she snapped, powering up the window, but not before she added, "Just watch out for her husband. Bob's a big man."

He took a step back. Jerking the car in reverse, she barely peered in her rear-view mirror before pulling out and peeling away like a speed demon, leaving him choking in brown dust. Yeah, she definitely had a drill sergeant thing going on.

Welcome to my regiment, soldier. There's the door. If it hits you in the ass, fine by me.

Jack put his groceries in the trunk and slid into his BMW, thinking. But this time, it wasn't about the case.

He spent the whole ride to his rental apartment wondering about that spitfire, and just what made her tick.

Chapter Three

Valentina drove the two miles down the pot-holed Long Lakes street toward her home, bashing the steering wheel with the heel of her hand and cursing herself, the entire time.

She hadn't meant to go off on the interloper. In her mind, she'd wanted to calmly and politely inform him that the facilities were only for residents. *Not* go off like a crazy foreigner, spouting Italian obscenities at the guy because she was too incensed to find the proper English words to use. She *always* slipped back into Italian when she got angry.

Damn Antonio.

She cursed her ex for the thousandth time that day. It was his fault she'd been in a bad mood, hell-bent on destroying any man that had the misfortune of wandering into her path.

And it hadn't been the interloper's fault. *Tom* had been the one who'd rented the place out to him. He had no idea he was going against the rules. It was *Tom* she should've been at odds with.

She winced as she pulled into the driveway, thinking of the stranger and those dimples of his. Her heart fluttered in her chest, and she threw a hand up against it. She was an adult, not some teenager. Why did it have to betray her like that? Hadn't it already been broken, once before?

As she cut the engine, she noticed Michelle, standing at her front door, waving. Michelle had been her closest friend, ever since moving to this side of the Atlantic. In her early sixties, Michelle had relocated here with her newly retired husband a year prior to Valentina, only to have him die suddenly of a heart attack, a couple months later. Since then, with her children scattered across the country, she'd been living alone, in a cabin just around the bend from Valentina, on Pine Street.

Valentina climbed out of her pick-up and smiled as she noticed that Michelle was just leaving another delivery of tomatoes from her garden. Michelle may have lived alone, but she would never be lonely—she had far too many activities to keep her busy, gardening being one of her specialties.

"I'm drowning in tomatoes!" she said as Valentina approached. "I hope you'll help me!"

That was Michelle's way. Always pretending like her acts of goodwill were favors others were doing for her. Her hair was a low ponytail, pushed away from her face as usual by a sun visor, and her skin was tanned and freckled from working in the sun, gardening and landscaping the grounds of her house.

"Of course. You know how I like to preserve my pasta sauce. I have tons of empty jars waiting for that purpose."

"Speaking of sauce. I have a recipe coming tomorrow that's going to knock your socks off."

That would usually be enough to get Valentina's spirits up. Michelle was a great cook. Valentina was, too, and because of her business as a wine importer, always had the best pairing. Michelle loved experimenting with flavors and leaving gifts in her neighbors' mailboxes—usually something with a Southern flair, like Gumbo or shrimp and grits, since she was South Carolina born-and-raised. Valentina had always responded with either a wine of her choosing, or an Italian dish of her own. Over the past year, it'd evolved into a bit of a club. On weekends, they'd share a meal together and swap recipes.

Michelle met Valentina halfway on the flagstone pathway, hands in the back pockets of her jeans. She tilted her face to peer into Valentina's eyes. "Uh-oh. What's wrong?"

"Nothing. What do you mean?" Valentina swept by her and scooped up the tomatoes. All kinds, cherries and Romas and big fat beefsteaks. Michelle never met a seed she didn't know how to work wonders with.

"You have that thing." Michelle pointed to that spot above her nose, right between the eyebrows. "That crease over your eyes. My mother used to say that if I did that too much, my face would freeze like that. Thankfully, I have other wrinkles to worry about, now."

Valentina let out a laugh as she unlocked her front door to the delight and happy wagging tails of her two lab mixes, Dante and Luna. Michelle always went on about her wrinkles, but for a woman in her mid-sixties, she had few to speak of. She made it through the wall of dogs, dropped the tomatoes on the center island, and turned to find her friend staring at her, still waiting for an answer.

She looked away, busying herself finding a place on the window ledge over the sink for the tomatoes. "How's Rob?"

If anything could change the subject, it'd be talk of Michelle's twenty-two-year-old son, the apple of her eye. The two ladies often bonded over talk of their grown children's lives.

Michelle fisted her hands on her hips and said, "Don't change the subject. What's bothering you?"

Michelle wasn't one to let problems go unfixed. And she was a good therapist, with a way of drawing heartache out of people, getting them to open up and talk about things. So Valentina relented. "Oh, you know."

"Antonio? The wedding?"

Valentina nodded.

"Has Bea left yet?"

Valentina checked the clock on the microwave above the stovetop. "No. She has a red-eye tonight. I'm worried about her, going alone."

Her friend leaned against the counter. "But is *she* worried?"

Valentina felt that crease over her eyes deepening. Actually, though Bea did have a tendency to overthink things like her father, she hadn't said that at all. She had been more excited to go back to Italy and see the place where she'd grown up. It was *Antonio* who'd worried, planting all these what-ifs in her head. "She seems fine. Antonio's been giving me trouble. I don't know what he expects."

Michelle's eyes widened. "You think he wants you at the wedding?"

"No. *Dio,* no. He just wants to torment me, likely." She moved around the center island and put the kettle on for tea. She'd baked *sfogliatelle* over the weekend, using her pasta maker to roll out the dough, a very time-consuming process, but Valentina had been thankful for the distraction. Right now, distractions—whether it be from working, baking, or riding Sunny—were welcome.

"Oh, you made your little bits of heaven!" Michelle clapped her hands as Valentina laid the plate in front of her friend. She took one and nibbled it, the powdered sugar clinging to her lips. "Trust me. You'll be better when it's all over."

Valentina reached up to grab two teacups from the cabinets. "I hope. So, what is new with you?"

Michelle popped her elbows on the table and got that gleam in her eye. "Lola came by."

Valentina stopped pouring the tea and looked up. "Bad?"

"Is it ever good?" Her friend rolled her eyes to the ceiling. "It appears that now, my mailbox post isn't at a perfect ninety degrees."

This would be enough to make most reasonable homeowners' mouths drop open in shock, but it was just one in a long line of crusades Lola had gone on. The last time Valentina had seen their nosy neighbor, she'd complained that Valentina needed to keep her garage doors closed at all times, despite the fact that she'd only opened that side ten minutes ago, to pull out her ride-on mower. "I'm sorry. Will she tell Warren?"

"You know Warren's useless these days." That much was true. Ever since Warren's wife had died, he had been checked out. Michelle smiled. "Oh, wait. Didn't you hear?"

Valentina slid the tea over to her friend, slipped onto her stool, and squeezed a slice of lemon into her mug. "Hear what?"

"Rumor is, he and Tina Wells had a *thing*."

"Really?"

Gossip never had interested Valentina, but even she had to say, this was interesting. Warren Harvey had been their upstanding, church-going, bank-president neighbor. He lived in one of the flagship homes at the front of the development, a sprawling estate that could've been featured in *Better Homes and Gardens*. But after his wife died in a hiking accident in the Smokies on an anniversary trip, he'd gone off the rails.

Michelle nodded. "But with Tina and Sam gone, completely cleared out of their place . . . Warren's probably lost. First his wife, now Tina?" She brought the tea to her lips and stopped. "I guarantee Tina was the one who drove Sam's business into the ground, what with those trips and her hair-do's and weekly mani-pedis. No doubt who wears the pants in that couple."

It was true. Tina may have looked the part of the sweet, accommodating wife, but she had the personality of a bulldozer. "Poor Sam."

"Oh, screw Sam. If he hadn't indulged his floozy wife, maybe Long Lakes wouldn't have all those potholes and we could actually get the common areas back to normal. Of all the things Lola has to worry about, my mailbox post should be the least of them."

It was true. Sam Wells might not have done it all himself, but something had contributed to the Long Lakes development going bankrupt and being unable to maintain any of the common areas and facilities. Now, it fell on all the residents to take care of the place.

They tried to manage, but none of them had signed up for the extra work. "You think they made off with our money?"

Michelle shrugged. "Who knows? I don't like to gossip. But their house is empty, and she wasn't just a doe-eyed innocent. She knew just what she was doing." She sighed, polished off her *sfogliatella*, and licked the powdered sugar from her fingers. "And so the rest of the community goes to pot while they're out enjoying our money."

That reminded Valentina. "Tom's renting apartments to outsiders."

"He is? Bastard. How'd you find that out?"

That question was because Valentina was usually the *last* to find anything out. She stayed on the fringes, outside the loop, preferring to be filled in on the details by Michelle, who didn't mind entering the fray in order to stay informed. "I ran into one. At the general store."

Michelle's face twisted in indignation, but suddenly softened as she took in her friend's expression. "One . . . Wait . . . was it a man?"

"Ye-es," Valentina said carefully.

"A good-looking one?"

Michelle was sometimes too perceptive for her own good. Yes, the man was good-looking. Thick dark hair, trimmed goatee, piercing blue eyes, slim and tall, with a bit of a movie-star look to him, though he didn't precisely carry himself with the swagger of a movie star. The unchecked traces of salt and pepper at his hairline showed that, unlike Antonio, he wasn't trying desperately to turn back the clock. "What difference does it make?"

"The difference, love, is that you are still very much a spring chicken. And I don't think you should be alone," she said, laying a hand on Valentina's across the table. "I saw the way your eyes got. So . . . he's attractive? Single?"

Valentina shook her head. "That has nothing to do with what we were talking about, which was that Tom went against HOA—"

She stopped when she caught a glimpse out the window of a slight figure walking near her back fence.

Strange. The fence was a post and beam, offering no privacy, and it backed up to a field of grass that wasn't used for much of anything. In fact, she'd never seen anyone out there before. She squinted and realized the figure loping through the tall grass was Jerry, husband of Molly, from the barn.

"Now what do you suppose he's up to?" Michelle said, echoing Valentina's thoughts.

Valentina went to the sliding glass door and threw it open, stepping out onto the back porch. She cupped her hands over her mouth. "Jerry! What are you doing?"

He straightened and waved at her. Then he called back, "Just checking the fence for holes. Don't want the cows don't get out!"

Michelle had come out behind her, taking a bite of her second pastry. She said, "That's Jerry Vinton for you. If only he paid as much attention to their teeth as they did to those cows, huh?"

Valentina laughed, and together, the two went back inside. But something didn't quite sit right with her, and she couldn't pinpoint exactly what it was. In the three years she'd been here, had she ever seen Jerry fix that fence before? No.

In fact, she'd never seen a cow or a horse or *any* animal, grazing in that field.

Not even once.

Chapter Four

What's an Italian lady doing way out here in the sticks?

That was the question that kept pelting Jack's brain as he retrieved the groceries from the trunk of his BMW.

What he should've been doing is thinking about Sam Wells. The developer and the subject of this investigation. Though she was friendly enough, maybe even too friendly, Ellie at the general store had given him absolutely nothing to work with. That meant he had to find other people willing to give him info. People in the know.

People who weren't going to jump down his throat, like that little Italian firecracker.

Pushing her out of his mind, he juggled the grocery bag while fishing in the pocket of his jeans for the key, attached to a round bottlecap opener with an ad for *Tom's Properties*. Tom hadn't been helpful, either—in fact, he'd never met the guy. All of his dealings with him had been over email, and he'd left the keys in the mailbox.

As far as cases go, he had to admit this one was off to a rough start.

He pushed open the door to the dark, sparsely furnished one-bedroom. It smelled faintly of Pine-Sol, which was good. Jack liked things to be clean.

He dropped the groceries in the pass-through leading to the kitchen and looked around. Truthfully, the place wasn't much of a downgrade from the apartment he'd been renting in Nashville. Yvonne and the kids had gotten the house.

Everything was good now. He had a job he loved, where he could now take long-term assignments without having to worry about getting home for dinner time, or guilt trips for missing a school function. Things were just *fine*.

The apartment was furnished, though not well. Lumpy, burnt-orange chenille sofa, mismatched chairs, pitted fruitwood dining set that even most second-hand stores would've relegated to the firewood pile by now. Paintings on the wall that looked like children's elementary school art projects gone *very* awry. It was all well and good to Jack. He never was much for décor.

The rations, once put into the refrigerator, still made it look like that of a bachelor—he'd need to venture into wherever the nearest Piggly Wiggly was, soon, if he wanted to get some real food. Leaving out the Wonder bread, peanut butter, and jelly, he made himself a couple of sandwiches and sat down on the sofa with them and a beer.

As he ate, he opened up the accordion file for the Sam Wells case and started paging through the details.

He'd read through it all a number of times. Sam Wells had gotten financing for the Long Lakes development, situated on 3,500 acres at Falcon Lake, five years prior, and he'd gone through the normal routine to attract buyers. He'd thrown that financing into building a clubhouse, a general store, a pool area, a picnic pavilion, and a beautiful barn with paddocks and corral, then printed up a lot of fancy brochures for the log cabin homesites. But somewhere along the line, he'd begun to lose money.

Serious money.

Jack had been investigating bankruptcy fraud for a long time, and could now spot a red flag pretty easily. But one look at Sam Wells' financial records would've raised eyebrows, even above untrained eyes. In the past year, there'd been a number of massive withdrawals for the purchase of vague property services and improvements, that—now that Jack was here—clearly hadn't been completed. It all smacked of shady business and concealed assets.

And it was as routine as they came. He had to get the evidence he needed to hand over to the lawyers and get this son-of-a-bitch prosecuted.

If they could even find the son-of-a-bitch. He'd skipped off, too, leaving the residents who'd bought into the development to fend for themselves.

But that was human nature. Running away from trouble. Jack's wife had learned that, all too well. The second she'd even sensed a hint of it, forget working it out. She'd run off for the hills, taking Lily and Brayden to greener pastures.

For a second, he thought of Lily, in her white First Communion dress, all done up like a little bride. That was the last time he'd seen her, so pretty and sweet and delighted to see him. Who knew what kind of not-so-nice things Yvonne had poisoned his daughter's mind with in the three months, since? The last time he'd tried to talk to Lily, on the phone, she hadn't been interested. Hadn't said more than two words to him.

He polished off the sandwiches and looked down at his beer. Only half-empty, and it was already doing its job, getting him into a depressed state.

He went to the sink and dumped it out.

Time to focus.

He gathered his keys and his phone and went outside, to the other apartments in the complex. There were three others, each one on a different side of the log building, so as to give them a private entrance. He walked around the building, ringing doorbells, with the idea of telling them he was just a new neighbor and wanted to be friendly. Unfortunately, no one answered. There were no other cars in the gravel lot outside; maybe he was the only occupant of the place.

Maybe the Italian firecracker had effectively scared all the other prospective renters away.

He went to the end of the road and looked out, in both directions. The houses were so far apart, he couldn't see a one.

Turning back to the house, he went to the garage. To his surprise, it wasn't locked. Inside, he found an assortment of bicycles. He wheeled out an old blue ten-speed, tested the tires, and hopped on.

He rode away from the general store in a direction he hadn't yet travelled. He hadn't been at Long Lakes long, but he'd seen enough to know the roads needed to be re-paved, and a lot of the common areas could've used a good mowing. As he cycled, avoiding the many ruts in the road, he came upon a small timber home, with a long, thin dock stretching out into the lake. It looked like some kind of Alps mountain retreat, with a manicured garden and a number of balconies on the second floor.

In his head, he'd been reciting the script: *Hi, I'm renting the place up the way, looking to buy. Just wanted to introduce myself and find out how the locals like it here.*

As he pulled up to the house and parked the bike at the mailbox, he thought of the firecracker and adjusted the script, removing the part about renting.

Almost before he knocked at the front door, dogs began to bark. He paused with his hand ready to rap on the door, and noticed that whoever lived here had a small herb garden on the side of the porch, and a love for travertine tile. Tasteful, but minimalistic décor, including a small water fountain. A rustic sign above the door that said, "Welcome to Elsewhere." It looked very European, very . . .

Suddenly a thought occurred to him, like a fist to the stomach. But by then, it was too late.

The door swung open a second later, confirming his suspicions. He muttered a curse under his breath.

The Italian spitfire wrestled two golden labs back from the door, scolding them in Italian, and kinder than he'd been scolded at the general store. Once they ran off, she stared back at him, hands on hips, eyebrow raised, like, *Well?*

Eager to calm her down before a second explosion, he held his palms up. "Nice dogs. What are their names?"

She hesitated, holding onto the door like she didn't know whether to answer, or slam it in his face.

Well, of course. She probably thought he had followed her. That he was some kind of stalker. "I'm sorry. I didn't know you lived here. Honest. I was just on my bike . . ."

Her expression morphed from annoyance to doubt. "Well, I do." Her voice was calmer now. "What do you want?"

As he stared at her, his script went out the window, and he fidgeted from foot to foot like a teenager. He didn't bother flashing the charming smile. It'd already had absolutely no effect on her. "I was just out riding my bike. Like I said, I'm looking to buy. And I wanted to get a feel for the neighborhood."

Though he stood a half-a-head taller than her, she stared him down in such a way that made him think she knew better and could smell his lie a mile away. For a second, he thought she might snap on him again.

Instead, she sighed and gestured toward the street. "You see the roads. That streetlight hasn't worked in a year. If you can look past that, maybe you'll like it. People are nice here."

She started to close the door, but he lunged forward, holding it open. "Wait."

Her eyes widened in surprise and her breath caught. He'd frightened her.

He quickly moved away to show her he meant no harm. "Sorry . . . why is that? I mean, why is the upkeep not happening? Something wrong with the HOA?" he asked.

"The developer went bankrupt. That's all I know," she said, shrugging.

"Bankrupt?"

She nodded. "Yes. Now, if you'll excuse me . . ."

He hadn't wanted to leave, now that he'd seen her during less excitable times. But she was clearly in the middle of something. "Yeah. I got it. Take care."

He stepped from her porch and stuck to the path, in case she was one of *those* who didn't like strangers walking on her nicely mown lawn. Before he got to the driveway, she called, "Wait."

He whirled.

She stepped out of the house, closing the door behind her, her hands tucked into the back pockets of her jeans. Her voice was low. "I just wanted to apologize for how I acted at the store, Mr. . . ."

"Erikson. Jack Erikson. Just call me Jack." He reached out a hand.

This time, she shook it. "Jack. I'm Valentina. I was having a bit of a bad day. My husband—" She stopped, and waved it away. "It doesn't matter. Anyway, it's nice to meet you."

This was progress, at least. But it was a damn shame she was married. He felt a little flash of envy for this man he'd never met. "Well, husbands sometimes have that effect on their wives."

She winced. "I meant, my *ex*-husband. He's remarrying in Milan, and I'm sending my daughter there for the wedding this weekend."

"Ah." He didn't know why he was happy to hear it. He didn't plan on doing anything with that bit of information. At least, he didn't *want* to. "Sounds like you have a lot on your mind."

"Yes. I do. Anyway, again, I'm sorry." She actually managed a bit of a smile, which, small though it was, transformed her face. It made her even more beautiful.

"No worries." He started to back away, nearly tripping over a hosta plant on the walk.

"Oh, Jack?" she said, and he snapped his attention to hers at once. "If you are looking for information about Long Lakes, you should try Lola Edwards. She lives on the other side of the store, but usually, around this time of the day, you'll find her at the pool. She has her nose in just about *everything*."

So maybe things were starting to turn around. Jack grinned. "Thanks. I'll do that."

Valentina tilted her head. "You really are thinking of buying around here?"

She said it in a way that made Jack think she doubted his every word. "Of course. It's charming here." He rubbed the back of his neck, which was damp with sweat from the mid-day heat. "Why else would I care?"

"You said you were writing a book."

"I did?"

She nodded. "I thought this might be . . ." she paused, as if trying to think of the right word. "Research?"

He shook his head. "Oh. No. My book is a fantasy. A novel. It's all straight out of my imagination. I just figured the peace and quiet would do me good."

"Oh?" She smiled, a smile that held a meaning he couldn't quite make out. "How nice."

He wasn't sure she meant that. It was like she knew it was all a ruse, from the second he'd stepped into her orbit. There was something so perceptive about her, the way her light, Elizabeth Taylor-eyes assessed him, that told of a thousand thoughts churning in her head. She seemed to easily read his mind; but Jack? Jack had no idea what was going on in hers.

Then she reached for her phone and started to thumb something in. "If you give me your number, I'll text you mine. If you want a tour, I'll be happy to show you around."

"That would be great." He recited the number to her. This was definite progress in the right direction. "I can text you tomorrow?"

She shrugged like it made no difference to her.

"Well, I'll see you around," he said, turning, and this time, he *did* trip over the hosta plant.

As he made it to the bicycle, she was still standing there, watching him. He waved at her, and she waved back, but he couldn't shake the feeling that crept over him.

Nice job, Jack. You've been undercover here for all of three hours and already the locals are suspicious of you.

Well, not all of them. Just one, in particular.

But unfortunately, he had a feeling she was the one that mattered most.

Chapter Five

Acting upon Valentina's advice, Jack rode his borrowed bicycle back to the front of the development, across from the general store, where he'd seen the sprawling recreation clubhouse and fenced-in pool complex.

The parking lot was fairly empty, probably because, despite the heat, clouds had rolled in, threatening rain.

As he steered the bike into the metal rack outside the pool house, he heard the whistle of the lifeguard and the sound of shrieking kids.

The scent of chlorine hung heavy in the humid air as he went through the archway of the pool house, past the picnic tables, to the open gate. There was a sign that said, *No one permitted in pool area without badge,* and a station at the front of the gate, but it was unmanned. Jack walked through to see a bored-looking teenager in mirrored sunglasses, twirling the string of his whistle around his finger and staring down at the kidney-shaped pool from his perch. A couple of kids splashed in the shallow end, but other than that, the pool was empty.

Most of the lounge chairs on the patio area were unoccupied, but if they were filled, it was by older types. Even the little kids were being looked after by what appeared to be their grandparents. It was mid-day, on a workday, so that made sense.

It didn't take Sherlock to determine Lola's crowd, an explosion of peacock-bright colors and loud laughter. The six or so ladies noticed him right away, tilting their sunglasses down and craning their necks to get a better look. One said something, and the rest giggled. A gaggle of teenagers, only in one-piece, tummy-toning swimwear instead of bikinis.

Removing his sunglasses, he walked toward them, and their eyes followed his every step.

"Good afternoon, ladies," he said, flashing that charming smile. "I'm looking for Lola Edwards?"

A fifty-something woman in a hot pink bathing suit and a perfectly coiffed red bob patted her chest, one manicured finger significantly weighed-down by a massive diamond wedding ring. Jack could just imagine her batting falsies behind those cat's-eye sunglasses of hers as she said in a Scarlet O'Hara drawl, "Why, me? What does a man like you want with little ol' me? Am I in trouble?"

The group laughed as if it were happy hour at the comedy club.

He thought so. In their tightly-closed group, thick with the scent of competing perfumes, she was the sun all the other planets orbited around. Jack had a feeling he'd wandered into hostile territory as he cleared his throat. "I'm looking to buy in this neighborhood, and a little bird told me you know everything about this place."

She beamed at him, clearly flattered. "I *do* know quite a bit. Who told you?" She pulled off her glasses, revealing thickly made-up eyes, as he'd expected, narrowed at him. "Was it Andy at the clubhouse? Molly at the stables?"

He started to shrug when a voice said, "Hello, Jack. Funny bumping into you again!"

All heads swung in the direction of Ellie, who was lying out, zinc oxide slathered over her nose. Despite her concern for the skin on her face, her pale skin appeared to be growing rather red and blotchy, especially on the chest. She winked at him.

"Hello, Ellie."

Lola clearly didn't like the idea of losing attention to Ellie, or the fact that Ellie knew something before she did. The next time she spoke, she'd lost the accommodating southern drawl. "Who's your friend, Ellie? And why didn't you tell us about him?"

Ellie giggled nervously. "Oh. Sorry. I didn't get a chance to. Jack and I met at the general store this morning. He's a *writer*." She whispered the last part, as if it was some dirty profession, like male stripper.

Lola's painted lips made the shape of an O. "Is that so? Well, *Jack . . .*"

He reached out his hand. "Jack Erikson. Pleased to meet you."

She shook his hand with only the tips of hers, her long fingernails scratching his palm. "Delighted, Mr. Erikson. That name sounds like a writer's name. And you look like one, too, doesn't he girls?" They all nodded in unison, her eager disciples. "Let me guess? A travel magazine?"

Ellie shook her head, obviously gleeful over knowing something the others didn't. "He writes *fantasy*." Again, with the low, "dirty-word" voice.

"Ah." Lola nodded. The rest of the women nodded, too. From the Nora Roberts sticking out of her beach bag, the assortment of fashion magazines on the other ladies' laps, and the *Big Little Lies* on the side table between two lounges, Jack got the feeling this revelation would bring the conversation to a screeching halt. But he'd underestimated Lola. "You must be a very talented man. You'd be a great asset to our friendly little community, I'm sure. You arrived just today, then?"

"Yes, I—"

"He's renting one of *Tom's apartments*," Ellie interrupted, and Jack had to wonder if everything she said, she'd finish in that way, like she was throwing around dirty gossip about him. Which was odd since he was *right there*.

"Oh?" Lola tapped her chin. Jack expected her to react like Valentina had, but she didn't bat an eyelash. "Who have you spoken to already, other than Ellie, Sweetheart?"

"Well, I—"

"He practically got *assaulted by Valentina.*" Ellie, of course.

That raised every eyebrow in the circle. "No surprise," Lola said, unimpressed. *She* clearly wanted to be the only one providing the juicy gossip in this group, and resented Ellie's attempt. She leaned into Jack. "Don't mind Valentina. Closet drunk."

He crossed his arms and thought back to the woman he'd met. That didn't sound like her at all. "Yeah?"

"Oh yes. Bless her heart. She's gone off the deep end since that husband of hers left her. *Crates* of *vino* are being delivered to her house, almost every day."

Heads around the circle bobbed in agreement.

"And what about that neighbor of hers? Going MIA for weekends on end to meet up with that lover of hers, in Cookeville," Lola said, shaking her head with disapproval. "Last week she was gone *four days*. Her lawn looked like the Amazon. Just unkempt, unruly, unwelcome in a place like this, where we're all doing our best to keep things neat. I eventually had to go up to her and tell her that if she's going to live like that, she might be better moving into a trailer park in town."

The rest of the women listened, rapt, as Lola spoke. Jack had begun to zone out. Someone else said, "And what did Michelle say about that?"

Lola inspected her fingernails. "Oh, you know Michelle. 'Thanks a lot, I'll take it under consideration', blah blah blah." She rolled her eyes. "It's unfortunate she doesn't have a husband, but that's neither here nor there. I'm telling you, if Warren doesn't do something, soon, I'm going to have no choice but to file a formal written complaint and alert my attorneys. I mean, what else is a girl to do?"

The women nodded.

Lola made a clucking sound with her tongue. "I swear, I don't have time for that kind of nonsense. My baby's just not herself. She's probably going to need surgery, and it's worrying me sick."

Jack cleared his throat. "I'm sorry. You have children?"

"No. Buttercup's my horse. I've been spending most of my free time at the stables with Molly. She says she thinks it's something called founder, but I don't trust her. The Vintons at the stables? Watch out for them." She leaned in even closer to Jack, so close she was nearly falling off her lounge chair, and whispered, "*Spies.*"

He stared at her. Ellie's dirty-word disease appeared to be catching. "Who is this . . . Warren?"

"Oh. HOA president. He lives over that way." She pointed vaguely. "First house on Bluff Road. But warning! He's another one, bless his heart. Nice guy, but . . . you know. Men. Always think the grass is greener, but then they find out too late, they're useless without their other half. If you know what I mean? I'm not one to tell people their own business, but . . ." She clucked her tongue.

Jack didn't quite understand, because the woman was talking a mile a minute, but he nodded along anyway. "Thanks. So he's divorced?"

Her eyes widened. She patted her chest. "No! Oh, it was a year or two, now. His wife . . . Annie? She *died.*" She leaned in and whispered, "Hiking accident. So they say."

One of the women reached over and slapped her arm lightly. "Oh, you stop with the rumors! Stirring the pot!"

Lola shrugged. "The pot stirs itself sometimes."

"All right," Jack said. "Thanks. Maybe I'll ask him if he knows of any properties coming up on the market."

Lola reached for a giant hot pink cooler-bottle of drink, wrapped her lips around the straw, and took a sip. "You'd be welcome. You have that look about you, of someone who actually cares a lick about the appearance of his property." She wiggled her fingers at him. "Come on back, now, if you have any more questions!"

He nodded at her, and the rest of the group. "Ladies."

The moment he stepped away, Lola said something low, under her breath, and the group broke out giggling.

He walked faster, sure he didn't want to know what that was all about.

He didn't have trouble finding the house on Bluff Road. It was a stately mansion, even bigger than Valentina's; the kind of builder's model home that reeked of success and privilege, with a U-shaped drive and hedges manicured into neat but completely unnatural shapes. A shiny, decked-out black Dodge RAM was parked in the drive, with a TITANS1 license plate. Hanging from the lamppost was a sign that said *The Harveys* in a sparkling gold— probably 24-karat— script. Jack felt a little guilty, propping the rusty bicycle against the mailbox outside such a spotless property.

Even before he reached the front door, he noticed a man staring at him from behind the glass double storm doors. He had the look of someone who'd just come back from a long run—gym shorts, tech tee, shocks of graying hair stuck to his forehead with sweat. The man was probably older than Jack, but his t-shirt fit him the way it fit men years younger, stretching tight across his chest, instead of his belly. Lifting a defined bicep, he guzzled water from a Hydroflask, then smacked his lips and dragged a forearm across his mouth, all the while inspecting the stranger like he was a cowboy who'd made the mistake of walking into the wrong saloon.

Judging from the NO SOLICITING sign in the window, Jack was already on his bad side. He decided to lead off with flattery. "That's a nice lawn you got there. How do you keep it so green?"

The man polished off his water and capped the bottle, surveying his domain with obvious indifference. He didn't open the door, as would be the friendly thing to do, so his voice was muffled. Something told Jack that "being friendly" wasn't on his list of priorities. "I pay a professional."

Jack reached the front stoop, three steps made of cultivated river stone. In fact, the entire basement area, which would normally be poured concrete, was covered in that river stone, as well as the massive chimney. It must've cost an arm and a leg. "Are you Warren?"

Warren jabbed a finger at the sign. "We don't allow—"

"I'm not here for that. I'm Jack. Jack—"

He tossed the water bottle to the floor and fisted his hands on his hips. "What do you want?"

"I'm staying in one of Tom's apartments. I'm hoping to buy a place around here. Maybe build a house. Only thing is, I can't seem to find anyone to talk to about that."

Warren looked him up and down, one eyebrow raised significantly higher than the other. "You want to buy here?"

"Yeah. Lola down at the pool told me you might be the man to see."

The man shook his head. "I'm not. That would be the developer. Sam Wells. But no one's seen him in a while, so I can't help you. You say you're staying at Tom's?"

"Yeah . . ." Shit. He wasn't sure if that was going to come back to bite him, considering Valentina had said it wasn't allowed. "Just while I find a permanent place up here. Do you know of any houses coming on the market?"

Warren looked over his shoulder, up a long, sweeping staircase, as if something was up there that he didn't want Jack to see. "No. Look, I'm a busy man, so . . ."

"Yeah. Got it." Great. A dead end. He started to back up, Ellie's *We're all very friendly here* comment ringing in his head. *Friendly, my ass.* So far, he'd met far more of the type of person he wouldn't mind never seeing again. "Sorry to bother you."

He turned, and had nearly made it to the driveway when Warren's voice said, "Hey."

Jack looked over his shoulder, surprised to find out that Warren had finally opened the storm door and was standing on the front stoop, arms crossed in warning posture, his mouth a straight line. "Yeah?"

"You're the one who's been poking around, asking questions, aren't you?"

Jack stared. *Jesus. I've been in this development about three hours, tops. Word really gets around.* "I wouldn't say 'poking'. Just getting the lay of the land."

51

"Look. People at Long Lakes don't take too kindly to being snooped on. Catch my drift?"

"All right. I understand. But I—"

"They keep themselves to themselves. That's the first thing you've got to learn if you want to live here."

It felt like a threat. The sky overhead even darkened a little as the words hung in the air between them.

Clearly, you don't know Lola, Jack thought, but then the man offered his first smile, and not a friendly one. "Okay, *neighbor*?"

"Yeah." He returned the smile. "Reading you, loud and clear. Have a good day."

When he reached the bicycle and straddled it, getting ready to pedal away, Jack looked back at the front of the Harvey house. Warren was back behind the door again, smile gone, staring him down, like a threat that needed to quickly be squashed.

And more than ever, Jack knew that some questionable things were afoot in Long Lakes.

Chapter Six

One of the first things Valentina and Antonio had done when they moved into their new house in the United States was buy a massive king bed. In Italy, beds were smaller, and so was their bedroom, and so they often slept, arms and legs touching, if not intertwined. Antonio had always appeared to have a distaste for anything American. Garish, overstated, big.

But when they arrived in Tennessee for the first time, Antonio suddenly had a change of heart. He'd gone gung-ho for anything American. He'd wanted to go all-out on the log cabin. He'd bought the biggest pick-up truck on the lot. And he'd insisted on a massive king bed that took up most of the floor space in the master suite.

Valentina hated it, now.

The vast oasis of pillows and fluffy blankets was so American, and perfectly comfortable, yes, almost too comfortable. Valentina sometimes felt like it would swallow her up. And even covered in pillows, the bed was so very empty.

Even now, that empty space only reminded her of what she was missing.

His love for America only lasted a few months. Or maybe it was his love for *her,* the other woman, that overshadowed it. Valentina didn't know what started it, but whatever it was, it had started years before, and hadn't fully ended when he boarded the plane to the States. Shortly after he got to Tennessee, he broke down and told Valentina that he'd made a terrible mistake. That he had left a part of his life in Milan, one he couldn't live without.

At the time, she'd thought he meant the memories. His career. Their house in the countryside between Milano and Piacenza. The little garden he'd taken so much pride in.

She never expected him to tell her he missed Manuela, his mousy research assistant, who he'd been having an affair with almost since the day she started working for him.

He'd been gone for almost three years, and yet Valentina still slept on her side of the bed. She couldn't bring herself to stretch out and take up any more room, even just to spite him.

This morning, as the first rays of morning sun dappled in through the windows, she pulled her phone off the night table and checked the display. One text, as expected. Bea was very good about checking in.

Except, it wasn't from Bea.

It was from Jack Erikson.

It said, *Wondering if you're up for that tour this afternoon?*

A frisson of nervous anticipation made its way up her spine. He certainly wasted no time.

She moved to respond, but hesitated. Was she up for it? Did she even want to go down this road? It was so much easier just to stay home.

Instead, she got up and changed into her jeans and t-shirt. She went downstairs to start the coffee and begin her workday. As she slid open the door to the back porch—she always had her first cup of the day out on the porch, overlooking the lake—her mind was on her only child. Bea's plane should've landed by now.

The moment she set her cup down on the railing and settled into an Adirondack chair, her phone started to ring in the pocket of her jeans. She smiled as she took it out and saw her daughter's bright smile, looking up at her. It certainly wasn't the first time that they'd had a connection like that.

She lifted the phone to her ear. "What, are your ears burning? I was just thinking about you."

"Just a lucky guess," Bea said. "Don't worry, Mom. I'm fine."

That was something Bea had learned to preface every call to her parents with, because Antonio had always expected the worst. Valentina said, "Did you just get in?"

"I've been at Dad's for an hour! I didn't want to wake you."

She leaned back in her chair and frowned. She always slept with her phone's ringer turned on, just for that reason. "You could've. You know that. So how are things over there? Are you getting settled in?"

"Yes, it's pretty crazy. There's like a hundred people here. It must be all her family because I don't know any of them."

That made sense. Antonio didn't have much family left, and it was Manuela's first wedding. She nearly choked on the words, "I'm sure it'll be a lovely affair."

"Mom." There was a warning tone in her voice.

Valentina sighed and straightened her legs out on the ottoman. The sun was still low in the sky, so the air was crisp and cool, the grass covered in early-morning dew. The lake itself was mirror-calm, a thin line of dark blue crossed in the center by the narrow, wooden dock, with only a couple ducks drifting quietly at the very center. It was so peaceful, and yet no matter what she did, she couldn't seem to shake the mood she'd been in these past few days. "What?"

"You should do something. Something constructive. It's no good to be moping around all the time."

"I *do* do constructive things," Valentina protested. "I work, in case you're forgetting, which is a shame because it's what pays most of your tuition."

"Yeah, yeah, yeah, whatever, Mom," Bea muttered. She was sounding too American for her own good. "I mean, fun things. You know what they say. All work and no play makes Jack a dull boy. Live a little."

At the mention of Jack, Valentina's heart gave a flutter. "I know how to have fun. In fact, a *Jack* invited me out."

There was a slight pause, and then a gasp. "Mom. Are you serious? Someone asked you out? Jack who?"

Valentina cringed. Maybe she shouldn't have said anything, because now, she'd clearly opened the floodgates, and Bea wanted to know everything. Of course, she did. When was the last time Valentina had dated? Never, after Antonio. This would be the first time.

Not that it was really a date. "It's nobody," she backtracked. "And it's nothing. I'm just showing a man around the neighborhood. Possibly. He's interested in buying here. That's all. It's not even a date."

"It *sounds* like a date," Bea said, leaving Valentina to wonder if she was really so transparent. She understood Michelle noticing the change in her, sitting right across from her, but could Bea really gather that much from over the phone?

"How do you know?"

"Because! I can tell from your voice! So who is this guy, Jack? You said he's single?"

Valentina looked at the rafters of the porch, wondering why she'd even brought it up. "Yes. No. I don't know."

"Was he wearing a ring?"

"What? I didn't check! What does it matter, because it's not a date, and . . . I'm not even sure I'm going to go."

"You better!" her daughter blurted. "You must. That's the perfect way to take your mind off what's going on here. Do it for me. *Please.*"

Valentina clenched her teeth. Did she even have anything to wear for this not-a-date? What would be appropriate? She did a mental inventory of her closet and wondered if she could just politely tell Jack that she'd come down with the flu . . . forever.

No. Bea was right. She did need to get out there. Even if she had to force herself.

"Fine. But I still don't think it's a date."

"Even if it isn't. *Please* don't wear your everyday uniform. Dress nicer."

"My everyday uniform?"

"Yeah. Jeans. That big blue t-shirt with the lizard on the pocket."

Valentina looked down, glad they weren't Facetiming, because that was exactly what she had on. "Then what should I wear?"

"It's summer. Wear a sundress. Something off the shoulder, maybe. Show off that nice body of yours."

"Bea!"

"What? It's true. You can't sell if you don't advertise."

Now she was really regretting having asked Bea for any kind of advice. She really didn't want to know how much "advertising" Bea had been doing at UT. "I think a sundress would be overdoing it, *tesoro*. I'm not twenty anymore."

"Mom, come on. Stop saying you can't all the time, or you're too old for things. You're not even close to having one foot in the grave. You still have half your life ahead of you."

"I don't even know if I should do this. I haven't been out like that with anyone but your father since . . ." She gave up trying to remember. "I'm sure things have changed."

"Probably. For one thing, you don't have a curfew. So have fun. Do whatever you feel like. Sleep with him, if you want."

"Bea!"

"Come on, Mom! You should be having the time of your life! Hold on." Bea's muffled voice filled her ear. Then she came back on. "I've got to go. Dad's having some little gathering downstairs and they're calling me."

Valentina nodded, relieved to escape this exhausting conversation. "Have fun."

"Mom, you'd better promise me you're going to say yes to Jack."

She waited a couple of beats for Valentina's answer. Bea was stubborn, like her. She clearly wasn't going to hang up unless she got the answer she wanted. Valentina sighed, "Fine."

Bea let out a teenager's squeal. "I'm so excited! You have to call and tell me everything, asap!" she trilled. "I'm going to go down *right now* and announce to Dad and Manuela that you have a hot date."

"You will not," Valentina said, though she only did it halfheartedly. Actually, even if it wasn't technically a date, it wouldn't be so bad to let Antonio think it was. *"Ciao, tesoro."*

When she hung up, she scurried to her walk-in closet and went through all her clothes. Most of them were remnants of a life before—dresses and blouses and high heels—things she never wore anymore. Since she started this wine importing business, she'd traded all that in for, what Bea called, "her uniform." Maybe it was time to take some of it out, give it a whirl.

She pulled out a bright yellow dress and held it against her frame. As she did, she imagined herself, walking hand-in-hand with Jack to the edge of the pier, starry-eyed and content.

That kind of lovesickness had only brought her trouble, before. It had blinded her to what was happening, right under her nose. She'd cried herself to sleep so many nights, vowing to never fall victim to it again.

Shaking her head, she shoved the dress back into its place and closed the closet door. *Dio! It's just a tour. That's all.*

She picked up her phone and typed in, *Fine. Pick me up at one.*

Chapter Seven

Jack had woken up early, eager to get through his to-do list.

His first order of business was to put in a text to Valentina, and get that tour. He told himself it was purely for reasons pertaining to the case, but as he fixed breakfast and kept staring back at his phone, waiting for her reply like some overeager, hormonal teenager, he wondered if that was all it was.

An hour later, she still hadn't responded.

He'd gotten essentials at the general store, but his pantry was bare. Last night, he'd had yet another peanut butter and jelly sandwich, and didn't think he could stomach much more Wonder Bread. So he showered, intending to go to town to do some real shopping.

The second he hopped out of the shower, he checked his phone again.

Still no response from Valentina.

He thought he'd made some headway with her, and that she didn't hate him nearly as much as when they first met. Maybe he'd been wrong. Maybe he was still *the interloper.*

As he was pulling his t-shirt over his head, his phone buzzed. He reached for it immediately, but frowned when he saw it was just a notification from his calendar, reminding him to check in at work.

He called the Special Agent in Charge, Bruce Dees, a late fifties, no-nonsense, never-smiling former military guy who still had the buzz cut to show for it. On the verge of retirement, Bruce had just recently entered that phase of employment where he didn't give a shit, and was just trying to keep his head down until he could start collecting his pension. "Erikson," he grumbled.

"Good morning to you, too, sir," he said as he filled his pockets with his keys and wallet. "How are things?"

"Don't give me that shit. Just get on with it."

Dees wasn't much for small-talk, but he wasn't entirely a curmudgeonly asshole. He had a wicked sense of humor and was actually not too terrible to catch a few beers with, after work. And after Jack's divorce, Dees had been the one to provide the advice that had stuck in Jack's head the most: "Just keep your head down, and keep clocking those hours."

That's what he had done. What he continued to do, even now. Putting in the time.

"Not much to report. I've been here since yesterday. There's definitely something off about the place. Still haven't located the subject. No one seems to know where he's gone off to, but I'm following a couple leads."

"All right. Keep on it."

"Always."

He started to end the call, since Dees never said goodbye and usually just hung up, when Dees said, "And Jack?"

"Yeah?"

"Take it easy, all right?"

"Got it."

He hung up, bristling at the comment. That was one thing he couldn't do. It was idle time that usually got people in trouble, but for Jack, the alternative was worse. Thinking about Yvonne and the kids. So instead, he had a tendency to go overboard in his investigations. Last case, he'd hounded a subject so much that he'd threatened Dees with a lawsuit.

As he headed out to his car, he decided that this time, he'd play it cool. Get the information he needed to build the case, and get out. That's all.

He wasn't even thinking about Valentina when his phone buzzed with a message from her. *Fine. Pick me up at one.*

Energy surged through his nerves. He smiled.

He got into his BMW and stared at his hand, on the steering wheel. The gold band glinted on his ring finger.

Taking a deep breath, he took it in his hand and twisted it loose. He set it in the cup holder and stared at the mark left by it. The last time he'd been without it was his wedding day. Eight years, and he'd never taken it off. He shook his hand, expecting it to feel lighter. It didn't. Only strange.

Then he threw his car in reverse and backed out of the parking lot, heading for the nearest supermarket, which he'd learned was the Piggly Wiggly in Pikeville. As he drove, he tried to go through a mental list of groceries, but his eyes kept trailing to the ring.

Had he taken it off because he was ready to? Or was it for Valentina? Both?

He left the front gates of the community, down a long, narrow winding road flanked on both sides by tall, lush forest. As he reached a straightaway, he noticed a familiar black pick-up, ahead of him.

As he neared, he checked the license plate. TITANS1. It was Warren Harvey, all right.

He hung back, not wanting to get any further on Warren's bad side by tailgating. He expected that he'd wind up following him, all the way to the stop sign on the main road. Just as Jack reached down to fiddle with his radio station and turn on some Jason Aldean, Warren's brake lights flashed on, bright in the shade of the thick foliage overhead.

Without warning, he hung a quick left and headed down a service road. Barely a service road. It was more like an overgrown hiking path that *wanted* to be a road.

Jack slowed to a stop, thinking. He watched the truck, climbing over uneven terrain, before disappearing among the greenery.

There were a couple of problems with following. First of all, he didn't want Warren to get even more suspicious of him. Secondly, his BMW might've hugged the road like no other car, but it wasn't exactly a champion of off-roading. He tapped his fingers on the dash, thinking, all the while, Dees' words echoing in his head: *Take it easy.*

He should. He knew that. Just forget it, get over to the Piggly Wiggly, and do his grocery shopping.

But as Jason Aldean sang, Jack muttered under his breath, "That's the only way I know," threw the car in drive, and hung a quick left, onto the road. As he did, a cloud of dirt rose up around him and gravel pinged against his paint job.

For a second, he regretted it, but then he got caught up, thinking about Warren. Of all the people he'd met, Warren was most suspicious. There was something about him that hadn't sat right with Jack, from the start. And now, where the hell was he going? The Long Lakes community was out in the middle of nowhere. *This*—wherever Warren was headed—was like the abyss of hell.

Other roads branched off from this one, even narrower. Jack stopped at a fork in the road and listened. He thought he heard the sound of tires, to the right, so he took that path. Then there was another. And another. The black truck never appeared ahead of him.

Soon after, he realized that if he didn't turn back soon, he could very well be lost out in these woods forever. He'd driven up the side of the hill, and now there was a steep embankment on his side. All around him was forest, not a single sign of life anywhere. No homes, no prints on the path, and more importantly—no Warren. It was like he'd vanished.

Jack cursed under his breath and slammed his fists into the steering wheel.

He pulled forward, intending to do a K-turn to change directions, but the car lurched forward, front dropping, sending his gut dropping with it. He shifted into reverse and tried to back up, but the wheels spun uselessly underneath him, stuck on something.

"Just what I need," he muttered, having no choice but to shift back into drive.

He did, and as he stepped on the gas to try to dislodge it, the car suddenly started to slip down the embankment. He jammed on the brakes, but the car was already in a slide, and picking up speed.

It didn't stop until it'd crashed against a tree with an enormous *thunk* and the sound of crunching metal.

"Dammit," he muttered, grabbing his phone. He woke up the display and brought up his contacts list, wondering who he should bother now, but then growled when he noticed the words "No Service" on the top bar.

Setting the phone down, he looked out the window and dragged his hands down his face.

He really should've listened to Bruce Dees more often.

Chapter Eight

Valentina peered out the window, at her empty driveway, for the tenth time that hour.

Then, cursing herself, she climbed the stairs to her bedroom, took off the sundress, and slipped into jeans again. Better.

Though, not much.

She found herself gnashing her teeth as she took out her earrings and scrubbed the lipstick off her face. In the mirror, her reflection was a tight, pinched scowl.

Why had she even bothered putting effort into her appearance? And she'd been so eager and foolish, whistling tunes all morning and smiling so much her face had started to hurt. The guy clearly was a jerk. He'd invited *her* out. To not show up, without even a phone call . . . well, there was no excuse for that kind of behavior.

It didn't matter. She practiced relaxing her face, returning her expression to normal. How many times had she said she'd never let Antonio give her wrinkles? Well, this man meant even less. It *shouldn't* have mattered.

And yet something about Jack's manner had given her a small amount of hope, hope for the opposite sex.

Squelching that, she poured herself a glass of iced tea, grabbed a book and went out to the patio, overlooking the lake, to read.

This was fine. Better than fine. Comfortable. Exactly what she wanted to do. Her trusty dogs were by her side. The birds were singing. The weather was beautiful. Not a cloud in the sky or ripple on the lake. A lovely day to be outside, perhaps go for a tour of—

She found herself gnashing her teeth again and shook her head. Took a deep, cleansing breath.

As she curled up on the Adirondack chair and opened to the bookmarked page, her thoughts went to her daughter. Bea had been so excited for her and the big "date". She'd have to let her down, tell her that something came up. She'd be nonchalant about it, but Bea would pry and press and make it seem like it *did* matter.

Not only that, the *other* main topic of conversation, Antonio's wedding, would be equally grating.

Valentina glared at her phone, which she'd set on the table. For the first time in her life, she actually dreaded the thought of having a conversation with her daughter. She didn't even want to check her social media, which she often did, just to see what Bea was up to. It'd likely be full of pictures of Antonio and his bride-to-be, in Milan, surrounded by family and friends enjoying their wedding weekend. She wasn't sure which would be worse, her bitterness over Antonio, or her homesickness for the beautiful homeland.

She patted her book. It was a good thing she had reading material. Not that she'd actually been *reading* very much of it.

Sliding lower in her chair, she reached her toes out to bury them in her dogs' fur, petting them absently as she tried to get lost in the story. She hadn't perused more than a single sentence when she found herself thinking, *But Jack had seemed so polite. Excessively so. Not like the type to go back on his word.*

She caught herself, distracted again, and growled. "Valentina," she scolded herself aloud. "Get over it. He's *un bidonaro*. Not worth your time. He probably even forgot that he asked you to go on the tour. Which means you should forget it, too."

She'd read less than a paragraph when her phone buzzed with a text.

It was embarrassing, how eagerly she scrambled for her phone. She rolled her eyes to the sky when she realized it was just business, a winery in Italy, having trouble with the shipping company.

What? He says jump, and you jump, is that it? No, Valentina, from this moment on, you should never again let a man make you feel so foolish that you forget your head. You did that once before, and look where it got you.

Making the decision, she found Jack's name in her phone. As she pressed on the button to block his number, a sense of satisfaction washed over her.

Good. He won't bother you anymore. It's the smartest thing you've done all day.

Climbing out of her chair, she went to her office, a little room she'd set up in the back of the house. Her desk was in front of two windows that looked out over the lake, and caught the morning sunshine, so it was a nice place to work. Sitting down in front of her desk, she took a sip of iced tea as she looked into the problem, expecting its solution to require no more than a couple of emails.

She was wrong. Forms were missing, red tape was everywhere, and since it was the weekend, she couldn't get ahold of any humans on the phone. Then she found an issue with her revenue spreadsheet, and had to nearly redo the whole thing.

When her doorbell rang suddenly, cutting through the silence, she jumped as Dante and Luna let out sharp, piercing barks.

She looked around and realized that darkness was setting in. It was after eight, and she hadn't turned on a light. Blinking in the glow of her computer screen, she stretched her back, then wheeled her chair away from the desk and followed the dogs to the front door.

Before she opened it, she spied Jack's large form through the sidelight. She took a deep breath. *Remember, Valentina. He doesn't matter.*

She swung open the door and said, "Oh. Mr. Erikson." She was back to formalities now. "What brings you here?"

He saw right through her hardened façade. "I'm sorry."

The words, *for what?* were on the tip of her tongue, but she held them back when she noticed the bandage on his forehead. Not only that, his eyes were full of remorse. If he was an actor, he was a good one. So instead, she said, "What happened?"

He let out a self-deprecating laugh. "Mountain, one. Jack, zero."

She stared at him in confusion.

"I was on my way to the supermarket. I took a wrong turn, Valentina, on my way into town. Ended up going off the side of the road, into a gully. Of course, I was in a place with no cell phone service, and I had no idea where I was. I finally found my way to a main road, flagged down a passing driver, and got a tow."

She almost hated how quickly she forgave him. But she had to admit, it made sense. Cell service in the area was notoriously spotty, depending on the carrier, and when they first arrived at Long Lakes, she and Antonio had gotten lost on the many twisty, unnamed side roads, more times than she could count. "Are you all right?"

He touched the bandage and nodded. "Yeah. It's nothing. I tried calling you, but . . ."

"Oh?" She blinked innocently and looked down at the phone in her hand.

His eyes narrowed. "Are you having phone trouble?"

She nodded as just then, her phone began to ring, a call from one of her distributors. She quickly silenced it. "It appears to be working n—"

"Wait. Did you . . . block my number?" Before she could come up with an adequate defense, he said, "You did, didn't you? Wow. You don't mess around." He seemed impressed with her.

"Well—"

"Really. I'm sorry. I know you must be hating me. You have every right to." Luna was bumping her nose against his thigh, desperately wanting affection, so he ran a hand over her head, rubbing the scruff under her jaw. She was just as much a pushover as her owner, when it came to a good-looking man.

"Nonsense. I don't hate you. I'm happy you weren't hurt worse. You're fortunate. Those woods can be a maze."

"Good." He let out a sigh of relief, like her opinion was so important to him. She had to admit, he looked kind of like an injured puppy dog, fidgeting there, eyes pleading. "Can I make it up to you? Say, tomorrow at noon? I mean, my car's at the body shop right now, but we can—"

"Do you do horseback riding?" she surprised herself by asking.

He nodded, similar surprise on his face. "I do, yeah."

"We can meet at the stables at one. I need to exercise my horse, anyway," she said, adding an ambivalent shrug.

"Perfect," he said, making no attempt to mask his own excitement. "I'll be there."

He started to back away, and she began to close the door.

"And I really am sorry," he said before she could.

"It's all right. Take care of that bump of yours," she said, smiling as she closed the door.

She couldn't help it. That jumpy, silly, over-eager feeling—the one that only hours ago, she'd vowed never to feel again—returned.

This time, with a vengeance.

Chapter Nine

Early the following morning, Valentina placed a small glass dish and a bottle of Sagrantino into the basket of her powder blue Cinelli touring bike and headed in the direction of Michelle's house.

After Jack left her front door last night, Valentina realized she had to keep busy to avoid letting her mind spiral out, imagining their upcoming horseback-riding tour. So she found herself in the one room of her house where things made absolute sense, where she had complete control—the kitchen.

Valentina had grown up in the kitchen. In Milan, her mother and grandmother, who lived with her, were always cooking up treasured recipes, rolling out their own pasta, making it into a real affair akin to a party. She'd come from a close-knit family, and because her aunts and uncles and dozens of cousins all lived within the same area, there was rarely a night when they didn't all congregate around a massive dining table, eating delicious food and catching up on each other's lives. It was those memories, the memories of cooking and savoring those meals and those relationships, that made her happiest, and made the kitchen feel like a refuge.

So she'd cooked up a storm, enough *pasta e fagioli* to feed an army, most of it which was now stored in her refrigerator. Sitting down at the dinner table to enjoy the fruits of her labor had always been secondary. It was the process of cooking, selecting the ingredients, melding them together, creating something unique and tasty, that gave her joy. But mostly, it was the prospect of sharing it with others that warmed her heart, because it reminded her of days gone past.

But Bea hadn't been very interested in cooking, and Antonio wasn't very interested in food. Moving to America, where she knew no one, that was the thing she'd missed most—congregating with family over a good meal.

Thank goodness for Michelle.

She smiled as she braked at the mailbox, sticking straight out from amongst a wild array of echinacea and black-eyed Susans at the side of the gravel road. Contrary to the complaints Lola had lodged, the mailbox post didn't look very crooked. Valentina tilted her head, trying to gauge it from all angles. No, perfectly ninety degrees.

Likely, Michelle had gone to the hardware store right after talking to Valentina, and had gotten the tools to fix it herself. She was proactive that way, and never let any problem sit for too long.

Valentina slipped off the seat and applied the kickstand to her bike. Opening the creaking mailbox lid, Valentina carefully slid the bottle of wine into the slot. She was just about to place the glass dish in beside it when she caught Michelle on the front porch of her house, waving to her.

"The Food Fairy strikes again!" she laughed, power-walking down the driveway toward her. "Caught you! What delights have you brought me today?"

Valentina lifted the dish. "My *pasta e fagioli*. And one of the best offerings from a little vineyard in Montefalco."

"Ooh. Wine," Michelle said with a grin. She took the dish and dared to lift the lid an inch, inhaling its contents. Her eyes went wide. "Oh. Heaven. You are too good to me."

"Not at all. You just enjoy. It's the least I could do after you gave me all those tomatoes. I used them for this recipe."

"I know, I owe you a dish." She sighed, her normally cheery face darkening. "I've been a little hectic lately."

One thing Michelle always seemed to suffer from was an abundance of time in her retirement. She usually went around, looking for projects to do or activities to keep her busy. "With what? Is everything all right?"

"Yes. It's fine. Just this and that. You know." She waved the worry away, and the smile returned to her face. "Remember that dish I told you would knock your socks off? I just picked the ingredients up at the Piggly Wiggly last night. Creamy southern succotash! It'll be in your mailbox tomorrow, guaranteed! We've got to find more ways to use up all those tomatoes before they take over the world!"

"Sounds delicious. I look forward to it."

Michelle linked her free arm through Valentina's and started to walk her toward the house. "Come on. Let's chat."

Valentina checked her watch and wiggled herself free. "*Scusami tanto,*" she said quickly, "But I have things to do today. Another time?"

"Things?" Michelle smiled. "Would this have anything to do with the tall stranger I saw, leaving your house last night?"

Valentina's eyes went to the sky. Of course, her friend had been busy, but just Valentina's luck—not busy enough to miss Jack's five-minute-long appearance at her front door. The way she said it, though, she made it seem like they'd had some tawdry interlude. "Yes. That's Jack, the new arrival. Remember? I told you about him."

"The *good-looking* new arrival? So he is single?"

Valentina nodded reluctantly. "Yes. He's thinking of buying in the area and I agreed to give him a tour."

A smile began to spread on Michelle's face.

Before she could say another word, Valentina said, "Don't. It's just a tour."

"But it could be more? Maybe even a *date*?" Michelle asked. She started to count off on her hand. "Single? Check. Good-looking? Check. That's basically all you need!"

Valentina didn't want to go down this path again. She'd had enough, with Bea. "I'm not thinking about that. I'm just trying to be neighborly." Her voice was brusque.

"Fine, fine. It's just a tour. *For now.*" She raised her eyebrows. "Have fun."

"Enjoy the pasta," Valentina called over her shoulder, heading for her bicycle.

When she'd straddled it, she did a U-turn on the road and set off down the hill, the bracing morning wind blowing through her hair. It was still a couple hours from the hottest time of day, and though the sun was shining bright, there was an invigoratingly cool tinge to the air. She inhaled deeply as she pedaled out onto the main road and waved at a couple neighbors, driving past in their pick-ups.

Definitely a nice day for horseback riding, she thought. *If he even decides to show up. I'm not holding my breath.*

But from the way he'd looked at her, eyes so full of remorse, she had a feeling he would. If he'd really been all that bad, he wouldn't have shown up to apologize at all. That had taken courage.

Still, she wasn't sure if it was Antonio who had scarred her heart, or something else, but she wasn't quite sure she trusted Jack. She couldn't get it out of the back of her head that maybe his showing up on her doorstep, wanting to spend time with her, was all part of an elaborate lie. To what purpose, she didn't know. Even with that bandage on his forehead, and that puppy-dog look in his eyes . . . there was something about him that she couldn't pinpoint, something that just seemed *off*. It was guarded, not quite genuine.

That bandage doesn't mean anything. There might not be anything under it, a little voice inside said to her.

How despicable. Would anyone really stoop to that level, just to . . . what? To get to know her? Worm his way into her life? Steal whatever she had left? Maybe Jack saw her as a single woman, doing fairly well for herself, and an easy target because she wasn't from this country? Was that possible?

Probably just as impossible as a woman like Manuela, finding a way into the heart of a happily married man like Antonio. Four years ago, that's exactly what Valentina had told herself. *His colleague Manuela is so plain. They may work long hours together, but I have nothing to fear.*

The point was, when it came to men, she refused to rule anything out.

"It doesn't matter, it's just a ride," she mumbled to herself, wishing she could just leave it at that.

But she knew she wouldn't.

No, Jack had told her he'd gone off the main road while heading toward the supermarket, and that he hadn't had cell phone service. There was a labyrinth of wooded trails in the front of the development, just off the main road. Her favorite thing was taking Sunny on them in the morning so she could think, so she'd traveled many of the trails, preferring the one that went astride a small creek, because it provided spectacular views of the lake and the hills in the distance. If a person didn't know them well, it was entirely possible to get lost on them. Cell phone service was definitely spotty, there. She had a pretty good idea of where he might've gotten into his trouble.

Without intending to, she found herself biking in that direction.

That direction, incidentally, also took her past Tom's apartments. No sign of a BMW anywhere, which fit with his story, since he'd said it was in the shop for repair. Actually, no sign of any cars at all, which meant that Jack was quite possibly the only renter in the complex. Small blessings. She spotted a bicycle, leaning against the side of the garage, the same one he'd biked away in, last night. She wondered if he was still inside, and if so, what he was up to. Thinking up other ways to weasel his way into her life? Maybe he was Googling her right now, to get details on her. Stalking her.

She eased up on the pedals, lost in her thoughts, until she could've sworn she saw the front door start to open.

Not wanting to be accusing of spying on him, she pedaled harder, leaving the complex behind.

Really, Valentina. He's not a stalker. Get that out of your head. He's just an ordinary man.

Still, it didn't hurt to be careful.

She turned onto the road leading out of the development. About half a mile down, there was a dirt road. She drove hard on the pedals and crossed over the opposing traffic lane in order to make the left into it. Her touring bicycle had fat tires, which made it decent for the terrain, but probably not as capable as a good old-fashioned mountain bike. It certainly wasn't as equipped to take the hills and exposed rocks and roots like Sunny was.

As she went along, she kept craning her neck this way and that, trying to see if she could spot the place where his car might've gone off the road. The road was dusty and rutted with tire tracks, many of which could've belonged to his BMW or the tow truck that had come to his rescue. She remembered him saying something about a gully, so she hung a right to her favorite trail, which went parallel to the creek.

When she was just about to give up, she noticed a place where the vegetation had been all but cleared.

She moved closer and jumped off the seat of her bike, pushing aside dried leaves with her foot. Sure enough, tire tracks headed down the embankment, the victim of an ungraceful, unwanted skid into a place where vehicles weren't welcome. Branches had been broken and twigs snapped along the way. At the very end of the tracks, she noticed a large white gash in the trunk of a pine tree, like a teasing smile. *Don't you feel guilty for having doubted him?*

Truthfully, she was starting to.

A bird cawed overhead, and she grabbed ahold of the handlebars, ready to turn her bike around and get out of there before anyone saw her, skulking in the woods like a doubting Thomas.

As she did, she heard the sound of gravel crunching on the dirt road behind her. Then, a truck, growling like a motorcycle and then backfiring, so loud it made Valentina's heart stutter in her chest.

She knew that truck. It was Jerry Vinton's old Chevy. The thing was at least thirty years old, and a menace to everyone who lived in Long Lakes. Especially considering the way Jerry speeded up and down the streets in it. Lola, in particular, had said loudly on more than one occasion that she had no idea how that thing stayed on the road.

For a moment, Valentina thought he might try to come down the trail she was on. But instead, he headed further into the woods, down an even narrower road that even Valentina didn't know well.

Her attention finally swayed from Jack, to Jerry. *Now why on Earth is he all the way out here?*

Valentina had liked Molly at the stables, but her husband Jerry had always rubbed her the wrong way. Oh, he hadn't done anything untoward, necessarily, but it was a lot of little things that added to the perception, his possible drug addiction notwithstanding. He was quiet, skulking about the stables with hardly a word, so much so that he'd snuck up on her several times while she was grooming Sunny. He never smiled, but that could've been self-consciousness over his meth-mouth. And she always felt like he was leering at her, when her back was turned.

Add to that his little visit to her fence, the other day, to "keep the cows in place" . . . and yes, she had to admit she had a good reason to be suspicious of Jerry Vinton.

And probably very little reason to be suspicious of Jack Erikson.

Leaving the accident scene behind, she decided to bike up the unknown trail to see where it led and find out where Jerry had gone.

By the time she got only a quarter-mile down it, the monstrous, ear-splitting sound of his truck had disappeared. Either he'd gotten too far away, or he'd cut the engine.

The trail got narrower and narrower, until it seemed almost impossible that a truck could fit on it. Nevertheless, there were tire marks there. She followed it along, ducking low-hanging leaves and branches, and nearly didn't brake in time when she rounded a bend and came to his Chevy, parked right ahead of her on the road.

In front of the truck stood a small, clapboard shack with a tin roof, consumed by rust and vegetation.

Valentina blinked and looked closer. She'd never been in this section of the woods before, or else she would've remembered seeing this little shed, which looked like it'd been pieced together with any scraps of wood that had been lying around. It was a patchwork of colors and textures, something most humans wouldn't even attempt to *enter*, much less live in, for fear of the roof caving in.

Where was Jerry? Had he gone inside?

She stepped off the bike and wheeled it toward a thick tree trunk, settling it there among the bushes, out of sight. As she did, she noticed another truck at the side of the shed; this one shiny black, with tinted windows.

Warren's.

This is interesting. What are they meeting all the way out here for? she thought, crouching by a tree and watching.

As she did, her pulse thudded in her ears. Now, who was the stalker? But this was odd. Anyone would've agreed with that, that meeting in a place like this, in the middle of nowhere, smacked of illicit goings-on.

A drug deal. That's what she would've thought it looked like, had it not been Warren, the most upstanding member of their community.

It's probably nothing. This is a storage shed for Long Lakes maintenance equipment, of course, she said to herself, even though, she had to admit, it was a flimsy excuse. Why would a storage shed of maintenance equipment be all the way out here?

Just then, the door opened, and Jerry came out, followed by Warren.

Warren looked strange in these surroundings, dressed in his pressed polo and khakis, his hair neatly trimmed, like a diamond among a bunch of rocks. He peered over each shoulder, like he was up to no good, and as he did, Valentina shrunk lower behind the tree, holding her breath.

She peeked once again, in time to see Warren hand something to Jerry, what looked like a plastic bag. Valentina squinted. Her eyes weren't good enough to see that far. In seconds, Jerry had hidden whatever it was in the inside of his jean jacket.

He turned and headed for his truck. Toward her.

She sucked in a breath and squeezed herself against the trunk of a tree, trying to make her body as small as possible as the door to his truck slammed shut and it thundered to life. It backfired a few times before he threw it in drive, made a fast K-turn, and headed back out. A few seconds later, Warren's car followed.

When she was alone, with only the sound of the birds chirping and insects buzzing, she finally exhaled. She grabbed her bike and pedaled back to her house, not stopping once to rest.

She was sweating by the time she got home, but she didn't bother to get a drink of water. She barely bothered to pet Dante and Luna, who were eager for her attention. Instead, she made a bee-line to her phone and called Michelle.

Michelle answered at once. "Getting ready for your date?"

"Michelle, it's not a date," she said dismissively. "But that's not what I'm calling you about."

"Oh? What's up?"

"Warren. Do you think he could be . . . I don't know . . . doing anything bad?"

She laughed. "Bad? Like what?"

"Illegal. Like running a drug ring, maybe?"

Michelle was silent for a beat. "Drugs? What makes you say that?"

"Because I saw him, and Jerry Vinton, out together in the woods. And they looked like they were up to no good. You know Jerry and Molly are definitely on something, so it just made me think —"

"A drug ring? That's a leap!"

"I know. Probably. But after Jerry behind my house, working on the fence, or so he says, I—"

"I'm sure there's a reasonable explanation. Warren wouldn't do that."

"Yes, but—"

"But think about it, Valentina. Seeing two people in the woods does not a drug ring make. And Warren may have been having a thing with the developer's wife, but his face is in his newspaper ad every day with the caption, *Tennessee's Most Trusted Lender.* He's pretty squeaky clean. He was probably out there for some other reason."

Valentina gnawed on the inside of her cheek. Michelle was usually one to entertain the wild, gossipy theories that Lola came up with. For her to shut this one down, so easily, probably meant Valentina was being a little rash. "Like?"

"I don't know. The point is that you should calm yourself, stop being paranoid and start being excited about your date."

"Tour," Valentina corrected flatly.

"Fine. Tour. Concentrate on that. Have fun. And tell me all about it when you get back."

Valentina ended the call, poured herself a glass of water, and absently stroked her dogs' fur, feeling defeated, and more than a little uneasy. She'd called Michelle for corroboration, for validation that she wasn't going off the deep end with her suspicions.

But perhaps she was.

Perhaps because of Antonio, she'd never be able to trust another man again.

Chapter Ten

It rained a bit during the noon hour, as it was usual to have a quick, passing thunderstorm in the summer. At least a dozen times during the storm, Valentina peered out the window, at the fat raindrops splashing on the pane, and said, *Oh, well! Guess we'll have to cancel. Too bad,* with a strange combination of relief and despair swirling inside her.

But by quarter to one, the sun made a grand reappearance and the clouds had begun to clear away. The ground would be muddy, though not too bad, because of the ninety-degree heat. She'd showered, changed into fresh jeans and a short-sleeve, button-down shirt that tied at the waist, and gone through all the trouble of blow-drying her hair, so she was ready. All of her excuses were gone.

She took her keys from the peg board near the door and drove to the stables. Because his car was in the shop, she looked for the bicycle she'd seen propped up near the apartments, but didn't see it. He could have walked, since it wasn't too far between the apartments and the stables, but she hoped not, because she'd purposely arrived five minutes early so she could be first. She wasn't sure why she wanted to be, but it seemed to make it clear that this was *her* turf, and this ride was on *her* terms.

When she pulled in, she noticed Michelle at the front of the open barn doors, talking to Jerry. Valentina lifted her hand to wave but Michelle wasn't looking. It was odd to see her at the stables, considering she didn't have a horse, but they seemed to be having an intense disagreement. Michelle's brow was wrinkled in concern, her mouth a straight line. When on Earth had she ever seen Michelle look so . . . disturbed? The woman was definitely the glass-half-full type; Valentina couldn't actually remember her ever getting upset about anything at all, even when she'd gotten a dozen stings from a nest of wasps that were living under her patio. She'd actually *laughed* about that. Michelle could find humor in just about anything.

Except, from the looks of it . . . Jerry Vinton.

Valentina cut the engine on her truck and hopped out, heading their way. When Michelle finally did notice her, she managed a wooden smile and mumbled something to him. Then she said, "Oh. Valentina, hi."

"Hi. Everything all right?"

She expected Michelle to launch into the obligatory gentle ribbing about her "date". Instead, Michelle's voice was oddly shaky and detached. "Fine, fine. Here to see to Sunny?"

Valentina stared at her friend. Is it possible she'd forgotten? "Yes. I'm waiting for Mr. Erikson, as I promised I'd give him a tour of the grounds. Remember?"

"Oh. Of course. I don't know how I forgot," Michelle said absently, tapping the side of her head. She glanced at Jerry, who was also a bit red around the collar of his t-shirt. "All right. Church is out. See you later."

She meandered away, head down, without giving Valentina one of her famous, drawn-out, hug-filled goodbyes.

"What was that all about?" Valentina murmured after her.

"Nothin'. Uh, she was just asking about the boarding fees and stuff." Averting her eyes, Jerry rubbed the back of his neck and quickly changed the subject. "Uh . . . Val, you takin' Sunny out?"

"I'd like to," she said, watching her friend slide into her car, her movements clipped. Her tires squealed as she pulled out, too fast. They were the actions of someone whose thoughts were elsewhere.

And boarding fees? Michelle may have been a Southern Belle, but she wasn't one for horses at all. She'd been thrown from one when she was seventeen and broke her spine, spending the better part of a year in surgery and casts. Michelle didn't care a lick about the stables, unless she was asking for someone else.

But Valentina had a feeling that it had nothing to do with horses at all. Jerry was lying.

"You said Jack Erikson's joining you?" he asked, breaking her from her thoughts.

"Oh. He may," she said, not wanting to reply in the affirmative after the last time. "Do you have an extra horse available for him to ride?"

Jerry retreated to the doors. "Yeah. Maximus'll do it. I'll get him and Sunny saddled up for you."

"Thanks."

She gazed out at the road, wondering if that was premature. It hurt enough to have been stood up before, when no one was there to see her shame. Now, she had a bit of an audience, not that she cared all too much what Jerry thought. But the rumor mill churned, and she didn't doubt that if Jack failed to show this time, it was only a matter of days (hours?) before all of Long Lakes knew about it.

Just as she was thinking that she'd likely be going on this ride alone, a tall figure on a bicycle swept down the hill.

She sighed with relief as he sailed toward her, braking and effortlessly hopping off the bike before it'd even come to a full stop, just in front of her. "Hi. Sorry I'm late." He swung his long leg over the bicycle and gave her a sheepish look. "Had a flash of inspiration and I lost track of the time."

He'd removed the bandage, and there was the trace of a bruise there, in his hairline, so at least he hadn't been lying about that. He was dressed nicely, in jeans and a plaid shirt, and he smelled faintly of soap, so he'd clearly put in some effort. Checking her phone, he was really only three minutes late. She'd let him off easy this time.

"Not as late as last time," she said with a smirk, fastening a baseball cap on her head and pulling her black ponytail through the opening to keep it on, during their ride.

He swept his hand in a gentlemanly way, allowing her to go first. "True."

"Jerry's just saddling up our horses right now," she said, guiding him into the barn. As she did, Jerry emerged, leading Sunny, her pony, and Maximus, the largest, all-black Quarter Horse in their stable. Valentina smiled at the sight of her horse, took the reins and gave Sunny a nose rub. "Are you ready?"

He didn't answer right away, and when she looked back, she saw him eyeing the horse with a bit of trepidation.

"Are you all right?"

"Yeah. Uh, that's a damn big horse."

It was, indeed. "He's plenty gentle, though," Jerry said, handing him the reins. "Need a boost?"

He stroked his clean-shaven chin, sizing up the task. "Nah. I'll get it."

Valentina put a foot in the stirrup and hoisted herself up. When she was astride Sunny, she looked and realized Jack had watched her, as if trying to learn by example. "You did say you've ridden before?"

He nodded. "Sure. Yeah. Twice. In Boy Scouts, when I was twelve."

She covered her mouth with her hand to suppress the chuckle that forced its way to her throat. "Oh, I thought . . ."

"It's no problem."

She couldn't help but laugh as he made a couple of rather clumsy attempts to climb atop the massive horse. Jerry watched the whole train wreck from behind, unamused, as he was probably used to novices doing all sorts of silly things. He offered a few tips, gave Jack an extra shove, and by his fifth attempt, Jack had done it.

"You could've told me you didn't ride. We didn't have to—"

"Are you kidding? I love this. I've always wanted to do this. I'm good. Lead the way."

She gently snapped the reins and Sunny set out, onto the dirt road. By then, the sun was hot and she was glad to be wearing the cap to shade her eyes. When she looked back over her shoulder, he seemed to have had no trouble in getting Maximus to obey. She said, "How are you doing back there?"

He didn't look quite comfortable, but he didn't look completely like a fish out of water, either. In fact, with another few lessons, he'd probably be just fine. "Perfect."

"Is there anything of the development in particular you wanted to tour, Jack?"

"No. I'm completely at your mercy. Do with me as you wish."

She was doubtful, but she had to admire his willingness to try. Even so, she decided against the more difficult trail that rose into the hills and went aside the ravine, opting for a more level, easier pathway that stayed mostly near the road and the fields. She'd still be able to show him a lot of Long Lakes that way.

They rode for a while, down a narrow dirt trail, chatting about the weather, how he was faring after his accident, and when the body shop thought they might be done with his car. He said, "It's probably a good thing I don't have a car. I'd probably get the urge to explore, and what I really need to do is finish my book."

"And yet . . . you're out riding with me."

He chuckled. "It's a fantasy. My characters ride horses. This is research."

"Ah. So you've written many books?"

"Well, let's see. I've written . . . counting the one I'm working on . . . one. Actually, a quarter of one."

"And how is your writing going?"

"It's going. Slower than I'd like. But you know."

"Have you always wanted to be a writer?"

"Yeah, actually. Had a boring desk job. Nothing to write home about. Finally decided, if I wanted to do it, I needed to start now. So I decided to get serious and left my job. Hopefully I can make a go of it, but I don't know if I'm any good."

"Oh. Where did you work before?"

"Hey. What's that building?" he said suddenly, spurring her out of her line of interrogation.

She couldn't help asking him all these questions; it was that damaged, betrayed side of her that refused to take anything at face value and wanted to know all sides of everything. But she realized she wasn't being a very good tour guide. "Oh. That's just for maintenance. And back there was Bridle Trail Lake, which is one of the three lakes on Long Lakes. I live on Firefly Lake, and then there's—"

"Maintenance? Doesn't appear there's been much of that going on."

"Yes. True. Ever since our developer went bankrupt and split, we've been on our own. The residents volunteer for different jobs, minding the store, mowing the common areas, performing repairs. But it's not ideal. It's hard work, which was why . . ." She stopped short of adding, *I was so angry at you before,* not sure she wanted to remind him of that. She wasn't very proud of how she'd acted.

"That's a shame. Sounds like the developer really screwed you all over. Did you meet him?"

Valentina nodded. "Yes. Sam. He sold Antonio and me the house. But I haven't seen him in months. His house has been empty for a while. I suppose there are rumors."

"Rumors such as . . ."

She glanced back at him. Odd for a man to be interested in petty gossip. Mostly, it was Lola and her crowd that chattered about such things. "I stay out of those."

"How long have you lived here?"

"Three years. Almost four in October," she said, vaguely remembering when she and Antonio and Bea had moved in. They'd gone from room to room in the newly-built home, imagining just where all their big, new furniture would go. Back then, they'd been eager for a fresh start, excited about all the possibilities this new life would bring them.

Or at least, Antonio had been. Valentina thought he was tired of Italy. But really, he'd wanted to get away from his sins. Thought he could outrun them, leave them behind.

Sunny neighed softly, stirring Valentina from her thoughts. Likely, she sensed her owner's stress. Valentina loosened her hands on the reins as she realized Jack had asked her another question. "Hmm?"

"I asked why you decided to move to the States."

"Oh. We opened a wine-importing business."

The wine-importing business had been Antonio's idea. After working sixteen-hour days as a scientist, he wanted a change of scenery and "more togetherness", or so he said, and this was the way to do that. He was like that, though. Always having crazy, out-of-the-box ideas, pursing fancies and whims without a second thought. Antonio had been planning to work remotely while his position transitioned and as they got their business off the ground.

But by December, everything had changed.

Luckily, the business had done well right out of the gates. If it hadn't, she'd have been sunk. Having to return, alone, to family who told her she was out of her mind for following her husband's schemes. While at first, she'd felt trapped because Bea was at school and they didn't want to uproot her, eventually, she'd begun to think of staying in the house as a way to defy Antonio, to prove she could do anything without him.

Besides, she really did love Tennessee.

"So, you're a wine expert?"

"I suppose, yes. I have some very good ones." When he chuckled, she asked, "What?"

"Nothing. Just . . . I bet you have a lot of bottles delivered to you?"

She tilted her head, not sure where this was headed. "I get samples in, yes. Do you like wine?"

"I do. I'm more of a beer guy, though, if I'll be honest. Did a bit of amateur beer crafting on my own in college, and it's still kind of a hobby of mine."

"And have you lived all your life in Tennessee?"

"No . . ." She expected him to tell her more about his life, but instead, he said, "Where does that path go?"

Sunny had already veered toward it, because it was their favorite path, toward the ridge. But she yanked the reins to the left to keep her on the level route. "Into the woods. Perhaps another time. I want to show you the marina, over on Casper Lake, this way."

"All right."

She waited for him to say more, to continue his answer to her question, but he didn't. In fact, several times when she asked about his life, he'd shut her down. That wasn't normal, was it? In Valentina's experience, people usually loved the chance to talk about themselves. Unless, of course, they had something to hide.

Despite that, the ride was pleasant, and an hour later, when they arrived at the stables again, she felt comfortable and relaxed, and glad that she hadn't backed out.

He extended a gentlemanly hand to help her from her horse, and when they were on the same level, he said, "Well, that was fun. And educational. Thanks."

"You're welcome. It wasn't a full tour of everything, but—"

"Maybe we'll just have to do it again, then. So you can show me what I missed this time."

She smiled. "Sure, anytime. I'm happy to."

He nodded, handed the reins off to Jerry, and then said, "You know what? On second thought, why don't we do something else? Like lunch?"

"Lunch?" Her eyes widened. "Are you . . ."

"Yeah. Tomorrow? Noon? At the general store?"

She shrugged. "Okay, sure. Why not?"

He grabbed his bike from the place where he'd parked it, straddled it, waved, and set off.

Valentina just stared after him, cheeks flaming and slightly breathless, until she realized Jerry was standing next to her, waiting to take Sunny off her hands. He'd seen the whole thing.

But who cared?

She gave Sunny a pat and went back to her truck, still smiling. No one could deny it, now.

This time, it was definitely a date.

Chapter Eleven

The following day, for the big "date", Jack was early.

Or Valentina was late. Likely the second one. It was normal for Italians not to be slaves to the clock, and she'd been working all morning, so she'd gotten a later start. A bit after noon, with her hair still slightly damp on the ends, she finally climbed into her truck and headed over to the general store.

They'd arranged to eat there because there wasn't much else in the area. The nearest place, Joe's BBQ Pit on Route 11, wasn't anything to write home about, and the restaurants in Cookeville weren't worth the drive.

At least, that was what she told him.

Really, though, she didn't want to have to be the one to drive him, since his car was in the shop. There was something suffocating about having to be in the truck with him, going there, coming back. Not that their conversation had been strained, the last time. In fact, it'd been very pleasant.

She just wanted to be close to home, in case everything went to pot and she had to make a quick exit.

She realized that point as she pulled into the parking lot and spotted him, leaning against the railing of the porch. Smiling and waving at her.

Valentina cursed herself for those trust issues, rearing their ugly heads again. *He's a nice person, Valentina. Stop looking for faults in him. Enjoy the date. And for the last time, stop being so nervous.*

She had been nervous, her stomach twisting all morning. After the initial exhilaration of the horseback riding tour had worn off, it started to sink in that he was after her for more than just her wealth of knowledge about Long Lakes. He was interested in *her*.

When was the last time that had happened? And when was the last time she'd ever even looked at a man in that way? Other than Antonio, she never had. He was her first schoolgirl crush, her first kiss, her first love . . . everything. And all of that had happened so long ago. She couldn't help feeling like she'd wandered into the mouth of a dark cave and was peering in, not knowing what lay beyond.

It had been enough to keep her awake, all night long, tossing and turning in her bed.

But as she neared him, and his smiling face, all those butterflies in her stomach went away. He said, "How are you still upright?"

She gave him a curious look.

When he straightened, she saw the problem. He winced and grabbed his back. She laughed. "Ah. Sore, are you? You're not used to riding horseback."

He stretched his arms behind him, over his head, and frowned. "Apparently not." He extended a hand to allow her to go first toward the picnic tables on the patio. "That's all right. I'll survive."

She went ahead of him and scanned the mostly empty seating area, looking for a place that would be out of the way, and yet not *too* out of the way. The last thing she needed was nosy neighbors, gossiping.

Of course, they would, no matter where they sat. Maybe the BBQ Pit would've been a better choice. At least there, they might avoid the scrutinizing eye of neighbors like . . .

"Yoo hoo! Look at who it is!"

Oh, no.

Valentina's teeth clenched as she focused on the Lola's gaggle of friends, holding court at their normal table, overlooking the lake. From the explosion of red and purple, it appeared they were having their monthly Red Hat Society meeting, of which Lola was president. Lola waved at Valentina, then caught sight of Jack, behind her.

Her smile fell, but only a fraction of an inch.

Valentina glanced over her shoulder at Jack, let out a sigh, and headed toward their table. "Hi, Lola. Everyone."

Lola gave them a thorough eye-raking. "Well don't you two look happier than a couple of pigs in slop."

Valentina checked her smile and pressed her lips together. She motioned to Jack. "You all know Jack? He's renting one of Tom's apartments to—"

"Oh, yes! We all know Jack," she said, reaching over and smacking his hand. "How are you, Jack? Settling into our little slice of heaven all right?"

Jack nodded. "So far."

"Good. Well, y'all let us know if we can do anything for you now," she said, speaking mostly to Jack. "Me and my girls, we kind of have a welcoming committee. Don't we girls? We're putting something special together for you, Honey."

Valentina frowned. She'd never heard of that committee. She sure hadn't received anything from them when she and Antonio moved in, and they'd been permanent residents, not simply renters. Not that she cared all that much. She'd never once aspired to be a part of their little club.

She started to spin. "Well, I'll let you girls enjoy your lunch."

"Y'all have a good time," Lola said with that distinctive lilt in her voice. Even though Valentina's back was turned, she could feel the woman's eyes scraping over her.

Suddenly she had a new requirement for their lunch seating: getting as far away from that group as possible.

She marched to a seat that was near the general store, partially hidden behind a wall. As she did, the group behind them broke into raucous laughter. Lola's voice rose above it all, "*I said to my husband, he's about as useful as a steering wheel on a mule!*"

Valentina shuddered. Well, at least they weren't talking about her.

Not yet, anyway.

Next to her, Jack whispered, "Say. How would you like to eat indoors?"

She smiled up at him, grateful. "Perfect."

The indoor dining area wasn't quite as special. A bit cramped, it was sectioned off from the general store area by a low wall, and there was just one window, surrounded by various photographs from around Long Lakes. It was also close to the kitchen, but the noise of clanging pots and dishes was nowhere near as disconcerting as what was outside.

Now that they had gone safely out of earshot, Valentina had no doubt that their mouths were probably flapping, coming up with all sorts of reasons why she and Jack were together. All of them, likely so outlandish and unflattering that they wouldn't dare repeat them to her face.

But that was all right. Valentina had grown up in a big family, with many siblings and no shortage of taunts and insults being hurled about. She could withstand it.

He pulled out a chair for her, and she sat and took one of the menus from among the condiments.

"So," he said, opening his own menu. "You eat here often?"

"Never, actually." She scanned the offerings, deciding on a salad. She motioned outside. "For certain reasons."

He chuckled. "I understand. Lola certainly adds . . . color to this place."

"That is one way of putting it. So you've met her and her friends?"

"That's right. You told me that first day that Lola was the source of all the neighborhood info." He raised an eyebrow. "You neglected to tell me just how *colorful* she was."

She shrugged innocently. "Yes, I might have done that."

"You sent me into battle, unarmed. That's what you did," he said with mock indignation, teasing her. "I still have the scars."

She laughed. "I'm sorry. I didn't know you."

"And now? So I'm not just a—what did you call me? An *intruder*?"

She winced. Yes. She had called him that. It did seem quite harsh, now. It wasn't as though he'd arrived in the middle of the night, in a mask, to abscond with the community's valuables. In fact, he'd been respectful, through and through. "All right. I admit I might have been a bit unfair."

"A bit. So you wouldn't mind it if I actually decided to buy a place around here?"

More laughter from outside, muffled by the log walls, assaulted her ears. She wouldn't have minded it at all. In fact, she would've encouraged it, but she didn't want to seem too desperate. It would be nice to have another person in this development on her side, besides Michelle.

She simply said, "No. Are you considering it?"

Ellie came by with glasses of water for them. "Hi, kids," she said with a cautious look at Valentina. "I see you two are playing nice, now."

Valentina shifted uncomfortably, recalling the scene she'd made the last time she was here. "Hi, Ellie. I'll stick with the water and have the garden salad. House dressing."

"Burger and fries," he said, trying to hand the menu off to Ellie before following Valentina's lead and sticking it back among the condiments. As Ellie moved off, he laced his fingers in front of him. "What can I say? I'm a health nut."

Valentina laughed. "I see that. Are you avoiding my question?"

"No. Why would I be?" He shrugged. "Like I said, that's why I'm here. I'm considering it."

"And writing your book."

He sipped his water and nodded. "And writing my book." He leaned forward. "Why do I always feel like you're a police interrogator, trying to poke holes in my story?"

She straightened, a bit embarrassed for being called out on it. "I don't know. I'm just trying to make conversat—"

She stopped when she realized his attention was focused elsewhere. His phone must have buzzed, because he grabbed it suddenly and peered at the screen. He held up a finger. "I'm sorry. I have to take this."

Watching him walk away, she sighed. *That.* That was the reason why she couldn't help being suspicious. He was a writer, and yet he had an important call? Didn't writers just work alone, coming up with story ideas? It likely wasn't a business call. So who could it possibly be? She watched him push open the door to the outside, the phone already at his ear.

Valentina. Stop. It could be his sick mother. Or news about his car in the body shop. Or even business . . . it could be a literary agent. It could be anything.

Perhaps it was just déjà vu of the feeling of abandonment she'd suffered at the hands of Antonio. For so many years of their relationship, he'd treated her like the most important thing in his life, only to cast her off when she least expected it. She knew what it was like to be treasured, what it was like to be thrown away.

Or maybe it was just what she'd seen in the woods, with Warren. She'd thought about it in passing, chalking it up to HOA business, but she couldn't help wondering what kind, and why he'd had to conduct it in the middle of nowhere. Warren, one of the most upstanding members of society. If *he* was up to no good, then who could anyone trust?

And she also couldn't help thinking that if Jack *truly* valued their time together, nothing would've made him look at that phone.

As the door closed, she saw him pacing about on the porch, deep in conversation. Then, suddenly, the door swung open, and Lola appeared.

Lola removed her dark sunglasses, her eyes already zeroed in on Valentina.

Valentina withered as she and two of her other ladies, Alice Shanks and Bernice Moser, headed over to her, still maintaining their tight ranks. She grabbed her water glass and took a long drink, bracing herself for the onslaught.

Lola slipped herself into Jack's chair and peered at him over the tops of her glasses. "Well, well, well. Look who's *quite* the dark horse."

Valentina crossed her arms. "I'm sure I have no idea what you mean, Lola."

She leaned forward conspiratorially, "How did you nab that one? The whole community's been abuzz over him!"

Valentina shrugged. "I didn't nab anyone, Lola. It's just lunch."

"Yes . . . but lunch between two attractive, single people . . ." She shrugged and looked at her friends for confirmation. "People will talk."

People, meaning you and your cronies, Lola. "That doesn't matter to me, because we just stopped in for lunch," she said stiffly, as thank goodness, the door opened, and Jack reappeared.

Lola stood up and waved at him. "We're off! We just wanted to say 'See y'all!'" she said brightly. "See y'all!"

He waved back as he approached, walking a little stiffly from the recent horse ride. "Have a good day, ladies."

He slid into the seat and Lola draped herself over his shoulders like a cheap blazer. "You two have the *best* time. Don't do nothin' I wouldn't do, ya hear?" She winked at Valentina, then whirled around dramatically and marched out with her entourage.

Valentina sighed and finished her water. "Is everything okay?"

He frowned. "Why wouldn't it be?"

"The phone call. It looked like it had upset you?"

He blinked, as if he'd forgotten it already. "Oh!" He nodded and patted the pocket where he'd fished his phone from. "Yeah. That was nothing. Just the body shop, telling me it'd be another couple of days to get the part."

"Oh. I see. That's too bad."

More doubt trickled in. Ellie came with their food just then, so Valentina couldn't ask the many more questions that were bubbling up inside her. Besides, she didn't want to seem too much like a police interrogator. So she clamped her mouth shut and poured the dressing on her salad.

He took a bite of his burger and looked at her. "You're really going to let those women rain on your parade, huh?"

She stabbed a piece of lettuce. "No, of course not."

"But there's something on your mind?"

"No."

"Come on. You know, I haven't known you long, but you're an open book, Valentina. You wear your emotions right where everyone can see. You're worried about something. So tell me, what's going on?"

She wished she could say the same for him. She couldn't tell him the half of what was on her mind, but she did have something she wanted to discuss with *someone*. She'd meant to talk to her regular sounding board about it, but the last time she'd seen Michelle, she had been so distracted.

Valentina dropped her fork and sighed. "I did see something rather odd. And I'm just trying to process it."

"Okay. You have my attention."

"Warren—Warren Harvey, the HOA President?"

Jack nodded and wiped his mouth with a napkin. "What about him?"

She leaned forward and lowered her voice to a whisper. "I was out in the woods the other day and I saw him, at this little shack, in the woods. With Jerry. It looked like they were being secretive."

Jack rubbed his jaw. "Yeah. That's interesting. Where?"

"Well . . ." She froze. Great. If she told him that, he'd probably guess that she was out there, checking up on his story about the car accident. She forged on, anyway, not meeting his eyes. "I was riding. It was um, probably around where you had your accident?"

He leaned back. "Really? What do you think they were up to?"

"I don't know. It's probably nothing. HOA business."

"All the way out there?" he said, voice doubtful.

So she'd been right. It *was* odd. She almost told him about Jerry, creeping around her fence, but decided against it. If she did that, she'd probably have to tell him about Michelle, too. And then he'd *definitely* think she was overreacting and paranoid.

"I'll check it out," he said nonchalantly.

"You will?"

"I mean, why not? Little shack in the woods. Sounds intriguing." He waggled his eyebrows mysteriously.

Valentina stared at her uneaten salad and shook her head. "I don't think you should go alone."

"What do you think I'm going to find, Valentina?" he said with a smile. "I've survived Lola. I figure if I can do that, I can do anything."

Chapter Twelve

After lunch with Valentina, Jack went back to his apartment, revved up his computer to check his work email, and sat there, staring blankly at the screen, all motivation drained from his body.

He felt guilty for lying to her.

You're undercover. It goes along with the job description, he told himself for the tenth time since he'd left her.

But the call he'd received during their lunch hadn't been the office. And it hadn't been the body shop, either. That was Yvonne, piling more troubles in his lap. She and Marc had a weekend planned in Asheville, coming up, and would he be able to take the kids, as promised? When he told her he didn't know because of his work obligations, she behaved in the typical way, playing the "deadbeat dad" card.

He'd about had it. It was like everything he attempted to do to foster a relationship with his kids over the few times he had them, she quickly undid. He had to call the Y to get the schedule for Lily's softball games, because Yvonne gave him little or incorrect information. Brayden had ear infections and needed tubes, so he'd offered to be there for the appointments, but Yvonne had kept him in the dark. And whenever he asked for permission to take them out for a fun outing, even just to McDonald's for a measly hour, she always said they were busy.

So of course, he was frustrated. Ready to explode. And if he did, he didn't want Valentina to see.

He dragged both hands down his face, then pulled up a picture of his kids on his phone. God, he missed them. But they were getting older, and too fast. Before, he was their dad, someone who could do no wrong in their eyes. That was changing now, with every lie Yvonne fed them.

But were they really lies? Maybe not. He was far from Father of the Year. Or Husband of the Year, for that matter, either.

It was funny to think that only four short years ago, Jack and his wife were each other's fiercest champion. She'd been his best friend, ever since they met in college, his closest confidant. He'd lost track of her afterwards, getting a little too involved in bachelorhood, until he woke up at thirty and realized he didn't have much to show for it. That was when his application to the FBI had finally been accepted. It was only after Quantico, when he came back to Nashville, that he reconnected with Yvonne, and the sparks really flew. They were married just short of his thirty-fifth birthday, and Lily came shortly after that. Brayden a few years after that. They had a happy life, a *normal* life. Ups and downs, but as good as anyone could expect.

He couldn't quite pinpoint the moment when Yvonne began seeing him as the enemy. It happened gradually, he guessed. As the stresses on his job increased, he began spending more time in the office, coming home late at night, leaving Yvonne to deal with the kids on her own.

Yvonne had always been a social type. She liked getting out and meeting people, and she didn't take to being the stay-at-home-mom, so isolated from the rest of the world. So wherever possible, he tried to give her the opportunity to go out with friends.

He wasn't exactly sure when or where she met Marc.

The other man.

It wasn't anything dramatic. In fact, by that time, he was so buried with his job that he had absolutely no idea that there was anything wrong. And yes, looking back, they had been more like roommates than husband and wife. One morning, she simply came downstairs and said, "We have to talk."

He'd stood there, his commuter coffee cup in one hand, keys in the other, ready to jet out the door to the office, while she batted around phrases like "someone else," "trial separation" and "divorce attorney."

Until that moment, his mind had been cycling through a presentation he had to give to Bruce Dees later that morning. He'd half-listened, nodded, and then headed out the door. It wasn't until he was halfway to work that he'd realized . . . this was serious. And he'd just walked out on the woman he'd pledged to be with for the rest of his life.

A person can go one of two ways when faced with a massive life change like that. He can fold over and beg for forgiveness, for another chance . . . or he can get angry.

Jack did the latter. He got so angry, he had to pull over to the side of the road and call her. Here he was, working every day to provide a life for his family, and she thanked him by cheating on him?

Regrettably, he said some things to her that only drove the final nail into the coffin that was their marriage. But he made it in to work on time to give one of the best presentations of his career.

It was only much later that he realized that those things he'd shouted at her, while he paced the side of the highway, only contributed more animosity to what Yvonne was feeling toward him, and that she would hold it against him, even now, to keep him from his children.

And damn right, he was bitter. Yes, it wasn't good to feel that way. Yes, they should've put their petty differences aside for the good of the children. But every time he tried to . . . she just dug in deeper.

He pushed away from the table, went to the fridge, and grabbed a beer. He used the opener on his keychain to pop the top and took a long swig.

It probably wasn't a good idea, what he was doing with Valentina.

Scratch that. It *definitely* wasn't a good idea.

No, there wasn't much about Valentina that reminded him of Yvonne. Yvonne was the typical magazine-cover Supermom, picky about having the perfect home, the perfect cut and color, who enjoyed her daily treks to the gym and spending her Saturdays in the spa. Valentina seemed less concerned about those material things, and more easy-going. She liked the outdoors, and . . .

He cursed himself. It didn't matter. The last thing he needed now was to get involved with another woman. *Any* other woman.

He'd fouled up the first one. He didn't need another opportunity to do the same.

Besides, he had a job to do.

Tossing the empty beer bottle in the sink, he decided there was no time like the present. He grabbed his wallet and apartment keys and headed for the door.

He told himself this wasn't for Valentina. This was for the case. Most of the threads he was following had turned up nothing, and this was as good a lead as any. Plus, Warren Harvey? Acting suspiciously? Jack had had an inkling something was wrong with that guy ever since his not-so-friendly welcome, last week.

He jumped on the bicycle and headed out, toward the front of the development, into the tall trees, following Valentina's directions. She'd blushed a little when he'd asked her where she'd seen Warren and Jerry. Yes, she was clearly a lover of the outdoors, but he also had to wonder if there was another reason she'd gone out this way. Had she wanted to confirm his story about the accident was true?

He thought about the way he'd reacted around Yvonne, when he learned about Marc. He'd gone into a tailspin, following her whenever she left the house, wanting to "catch her in the act", even though by then, she'd stopped hiding it, and had even told him that she was no longer in love with him. He'd needed to see it, to believe his marriage was truly coming to an end. Everything she said to him, he doubted. He'd gone half-mad.

Likely, with her own ex, Valentina had suspicions of her own. She'd been hurt before. If she *had* trekked out here to confirm the story, he wouldn't have blamed her.

Doesn't matter, he told himself, willing his brain to stop dwelling on all things Valentina. It would only take him down a path he didn't need to travel.

He concentrated instead on the dirt road, into the trees. His bike tire bumped along the ruts. Eventually, he came to the Y intersection, where he'd gone right, only for his BMW to meet its sad fate. Acting upon Valentina's directions, he headed up the hill, off to the left.

This time, he managed to keep a pretty good sense of where he was, so he wouldn't wind up lost in the woods, like before. It was easy, considering the recent rain. As remote and narrow as this road was, it was strangely well-travelled, as evidenced by the assorted tire tracks from various different vehicles.

Alarm bells went off in Jack's head, only growing louder when he inhaled and smelled something other than the fresh mountain air of rural Tennessee. The acrid stench, like ammonia or strong fertilizer mixed with urine, nearly squeezed tears from his eyes.

He had friends in the DEA, and often went out to lunch with them and heard their war stories. Drug manufacturing was rampant, with new operations popping up as fast as his friends could stomp them out. So when he stumbled upon the dilapidated shack in the woods, just where Valentina said it would be, he already had an idea of what he'd see.

There was no sign that anyone was there; no cars were parked outside, and the doors and windows were closed. Walking his bike up to the side of the shack, he propped it up against the rotting, moss-covered wooden boards, and peeked into a window.

A shade had been drawn tightly, but one of the glass panes was missing. He easily nudged aside the shade which allowed him to get a glimpse inside the shadowy room.

The first thing he saw was a series of glass jugs of different shapes. Sure, there were plenty of toothless, backwoods locals fond of making moonshine around these parts, but that wasn't all. There was a metal frying pan hooked up to a contraption with a Bunsen burner and a number of rubber tubes. It was all he really needed to confirm his suspicions, but then he spied more. Plastic jugs of acetone. Containers of store-brand cold medicine. Milk crates full of plastic bags.

Not the most sophisticated meth lab out there, probably, but a pretty substantial operation. *Erica would love to know about this,* he thought. *She lives and breathes this stuff.*

Just then, he heard the sound of tires, crunching on gravel.

Pulse pounding, he backed away from the shack and grabbed the handlebars of his bike, looking for a place to hide. A rock pinged against the side of the vehicle, echoing among the trees, sounding ever closer. In another second or two, it would appear on the road, among the trees, and whoever was driving would easily spot him.

Wasting no time, Jack dragged himself up over a rock and slid down a leaf-covered decline as fast as he could, hiking boots slipping on the loose earth. Pain sliced through his shin as he scrabbled on the hill, lugging the cumbersome cycle, but he couldn't stop. When he got to the bottom of the narrow gully, he tipped his bike down onto the ground, scooped some leaves over it, and crouched behind a tree, breathing hard.

From where he hid, only the tin roof of the shack could be seen on the ridge above him. He heard the sound of a large vehicle, coming to a stop, door opening, and heavy footsteps. A door creaked open and banged shut.

Carefully, he climbed up the steep incline, taking hold of an exposed root of a tree to hoist himself up. He didn't go far, though. Just enough to see the top of Warren's shiny black Dodge Ram.

So his suspicions were right. Warren Harvey, bank president and all-around good citizen, was hiding something. Something big.

He went back to his bicycle, yanked it out from under the leaves, and headed through the woods, away from the shack, trying to find his way back to the road. On the way, thick branches and brambles slapped against and dug into his skin, and he tripped over rocks and exposed roots.

Finally, he spotted the road, and it was only when he climbed up to it that he noticed his shin. His jeans were ripped, and the wound was bleeding profusely, blackening the denim all the way to the cuff.

He couldn't stop to tend to it, not with the chance of Warren coming back and seeing him there. He hopped on his bike and pedaled back to his apartment.

When Jack was safe inside, he quickly texted Erica, at the *other* federal agency. She, like Jack, was always working. She'd call immediately, unless she was in the thick of a case.

He went to the bathroom and looked at his face. He had a couple of scratches there, like he'd gotten into a fight with a tomcat. He gingerly stripped out of his jeans and surveyed the damage to his leg. Substantial, would likely leave a scar, but he could do without stitches.

Jack showered, then slung a towel around his waist and stepped out of the shower to find he was still bleeding badly. He couldn't find bandages in the medicine cabinet, so he'd have to get them at the store. Instead, he limped to the kitchen and wrapped the wound in paper towels, not that it helped much.

As he was shaving, his phone rang.

He put it on speaker. "Erica."

"What do you want?" She sounded more amused than annoyed.

He chuckled. "Why would you say that to your favorite person?"

"You only call me these days when you want something from me," she said with a sigh. "I know, I don't wear the right badge, but that's no reason to look down on us little people."

It was a running joke, between the FBI and the DEA, which one was better, kind of like the rivalry between the Army and the Navy, since they often traveled in the same circles. It was a friendly competition . . . mostly. "You had every opportunity to follow in my footsteps."

She laughed. "Now why would I do that and join the dark side? Besides, you know how much I hate you."

117

It was more than just friendly competition, between the two of them. He and Erica had grown up together, living right across the street from one another. They'd been rivals in just about everything, from who'd learn to ride a bike first, to grades and scholarships, to careers. Their families were so close, they were more like siblings than anything else. It was her acceptance into the DEA that had lit a fire under his backside to get in with the FBI. "Oh, you love me a little bit."

"Not even. So is Yvonne any better?"

He smirked at her mention of his ex. "What do you think? Same as always. How're things at the DEA?"

"Oh, they're going. Same as always," she muttered. "Busy. In case you didn't notice, there's a drug epidemic in this country."

"Which is why I'm calling you."

She groaned. "Please don't tell me you're going to give me more work."

"I'm giving you more work," he deadpanned.

"Fine." She wasn't good at hiding it. She loved every second of it. She was probably raring to go, on her crusade to save the world, one drug bust at a time. "Where?"

"It's a little community called Long Lakes. I think it's a meth lab."

There was a pause. "That's outside of Cookeville, right?"

"Yeah."

"Wow. There's been rumors of a major drug ring out in that area for years. Every time we think we've got it handled, it comes right back. We've been trying to cut the head off the snake for years. You think you found it?"

"Maybe. There's a shack in the woods full of the stuff to make meth, I think. If this turns out to be the tip you need, you owe me a beer."

"If it does, I'll buy you two," she said, and her voice was a little strained. Likely, she was already piling things into her bag for the trip. "I'll be there tomorrow morning. Give me the address."

"All right." He quickly rattled it off to her, and said goodbye.

By the time he finished shaving, the wound had clotted. He peeled off the bloody paper towel and tossed it in the trash, then changed into his boxers and went to the kitchen for dinner.

He wasn't hungry, though. Instead, he grabbed another beer and collapsed on his bed, in front of the television, where some baseball game he wasn't interested in was on. He watched numbly for a while, then pulled up the picture of Lily and Brayden.

Yvonne had told him, in the heat of an argument, that she didn't want the kids to know him if he was going to treat them like they were unimportant.

After all, that's what he'd done to her.

As much as he hated to admit it, she'd been right. He loved them, always thought about them, but when it came to showing that love . . . that was where he fell short. Maybe it was his own parents, who'd never been much for showing affection, either. Yvonne had called him emotionally distant, and he had been. He'd gotten so absorbed by his work that he'd taken her, and them, for granted.

In hindsight, he couldn't blame her for running off with Marc. He probably—no, *definitely*—treated her better. The kids seemed to like him. He was probably more of a father than Jack ever had been.

He drained his beer easily, and went for another one.

Maybe four beers later, he'd drowned his sorrows enough to finally doze off.

He was awakened by a sudden loud thump in the living area.

Startled, he listened, eyes adjusting to the moonlight, slashing through the blinds. At first there was nothing, but as he rubbed his sore neck—he'd fallen asleep with his upper-half at an awkward angle, partially braced against the headboard—he heard it again.

Throwing his legs over the side of the bed, he checked his phone. It was after midnight.

He got up and padded through the dark house, feeling the walls. He'd fallen asleep while it was still light, and none of the inside lights were on. Groping in the darkness, he couldn't seem to find the switches on the wall. He assumed he'd just left a window open, and the wind had knocked something over.

When he reached the door, someone jumped out of the shadows, diving on him.

Shell-shocked and far from sober, Jack staggered backward, crashing against the hard wall. All his air left his lungs. He managed to shove the substantial figure in a black ski mask off of him, and delivered a couple of punches to the head of his assailant, before the intruder wrenched himself free and tore for the open kitchen window.

Heart thudding in his ears, Jack raced after him, but stumbled over the leg of a kitchen chair, his vision spinning from his drunkenness.

By the time he made it to the window and peered out into the chilly night, the intruder was gone.

Chapter Thirteen

A few days after her lunch with Jack, Valentina stood in the kitchen, muttering under her breath.

On the stove, a big pot of sauce boiled away, moments from completion. The steam rose into the air, only partially sucked up by the vent, and she'd been cooking all day, so it was hotter in the kitchen than usual.

She waved a hand in front of her face and went outside to catch a breath and pick more basil from her herb garden. Once she had the leaves, she rinsed them, tore them to tiny pieces, and popped them in the waiting jars. To the pot, she added some salt, a pinch of sugar, a little bit of pepper. She tasted and stirred, tasted and stirred. *Getting there.*

She checked the clock. Fifteen more minutes. Then she went to the counter by the sink and checked her phone. Again.

Yes, she was wondering about Bea, and how she was faring in Milan, and that's what she chalked her anxiety up to.

She refused to acknowledge, even to herself, that she'd been hoping for a message from someone else.

Jack had contacted her once since he'd said he would go up to the shack and have a look. It was a short message: *Back from the shack. Tell you what I found soon.*

After that, nothing. Absolutely nothing. So by *soon*, he'd meant . . . when? Was that some kind of American-speak for *Never in this lifetime?*

Clearly, he wasn't thinking of her now. But she'd been thinking of him. Too much.

She didn't understand. They'd had a nice time at lunch. After her initial doubt regarding the phone call he'd taken, she'd begun to enjoy herself. He was easy to like. Despite the language gap, conversation with him came with relatively no difficulty at all, plus he was polite and self-deprecating, everything Antonio wasn't. He'd left her at her truck in the parking lot, telling her he'd had a great time and that they should do it again. He said he'd call her.

And then . . . nothing.

She was worried that perhaps he'd gotten himself in danger. But here, in Long Lakes? What could possibly happen in their relatively safe, hidden enclave? No, more likely, he was busy with other things. His writing. Working out the repairs on his car. Who knew what else? She didn't know him well enough to guess.

All she knew was that on his list of priorities, she didn't rank very high. It was like that phone call he'd taken during lunch had told her . . . other things meant more to him.

And that's fine, Valentina, because other things mean more to you, too. Like good food. Forget him.

She tasted the sauce again. Ready. She got out the funnel and started to spoon the sauce into the jars. She didn't like keeping sauce too long, because it lost some of its taste, but this would last her at least a few weeks. Fresh was definitely best. Maybe she'd even make her vegetable lasagna for Michelle, next.

As she finished, her phone began to ring. She peered over at the display. Bea. She smiled and removed her apron, setting it down on the counter before curling up on a chair in the living room and answering. "Well, it's about time!"

"It's been a total whirlwind here, Mom. There's been something planned for every hour of the day, practically," she sighed. As her mother, Valentina knew those subtle changes in her daughter's voice. Bea sounded like she was dragging.

"Oh? What have you done?"

"Everything. They had us touring all over the place, because there are a lot of guests who aren't from the area and wanted the full tourist experience. They were going to *Castello Sforzesco* and to check out the Last Supper, but of course I had to go back to the old house. The new owners are idiots. They got rid of your rose bushes."

"They did? *Dio!*" How many ages had she worked to get those roses on the side of the house just right?

"Yeah. They put a stone walkway there. It's nice, but it's not the roses. Remember how they used to smell? I loved that. I can send you pictures, if you want?"

Valentina pressed her lips together, noting Bea hadn't mentioned anything at all about the actual nuptials. Maybe it was a good thing. She didn't want to think about it, just as much as she didn't want to think about her old home that she'd loved so much. "No, that's all right. I don't want to see such a disgrace."

"Yeah. I didn't think so. And I didn't want to make you homesick."

"I'm not homesick," she lied. "I'm just in a different chapter of my life, *tesoro.*"

"Okay, fine. So tell me, does that new chapter involve a certain hot American writer?" Bea prodded, in a cheeky way only she could.

Valentina let out a big sigh. "No, it does not. This chapter involves work, food, wine, the outdoors, and plenty of alone-time, which I actually enjoy."

Bea groaned. "Boring. What happened with him? He seemed really promising."

As if he was a candidate at a job interview. "Nothing happened. We went out together a few times. Horseback riding. Lunch, a few days ago."

"Horseback riding? Lunch? That sounds so romantic!" Bea said with a little squeal.

"No, that's not what it was at all. He's just a friend." *If he's even that.*

Bea was silent for a few moments, in which Valentina could almost feel her daughter's doubt, seeping through the phone. "So when are you two going to go out to dinner? Better yet, you should have him over for dinner. He'll fall head over heels in love with you if he tastes your *ciambotta*."

"Don't be ridiculous."

"I'm serious! That stuff is legendary."

Yes, it was true, Valentina's vegetable stew was some of the best around. Michelle had raved about it, non-stop. Someone had even called it "liquid gold." But she wasn't going to go making it for Jack as some silly love potion. She had better things to do.

"We're not having dinner," she insisted, going to the window and looking out. The sky was gray and threatened rain. The small sliver of Firefly Lake, sandwiched by the thick foliage of the trees, was absolutely still, the calm before the storm. An insect tapped along the windowpane, buzzing loudly for a time, before heading off. "I have no interest in that."

"Mom. Come on. Yes, you do. You love sharing your food with people."

That was true. She did love that. It gave her so much joy to see the smiles on people's faces after a good meal. Even if the face belonged to a man who didn't have the decency to call her as he promised. She didn't need him, though. She had Michelle. That was enough. "It doesn't matter. He must be busy. He hasn't called."

Bea made a clicking sound with her tongue. "Ma, you know this is the modern age, right? Women don't sit by the phone, waiting for men to call them."

She went over to the jars and peered into them, then started to tighten the lids. "Is that right?"

"Of course. Was he the one who invited you on the horseback ride? The lunch?"

She frowned. "Well . . . yes. In a manner of speaking, he was."

"Well, then, duh, Mom!" she said with a laugh. "He probably thinks you're not interested in seeing him again. It looks like he's been doing all the giving and you're just taking. You have to invite him this time. It's the polite thing to do!"

Valentina stiffened, her mouth slightly opened. Invite him? It wasn't exactly a novel idea, but it was to Valentina. She'd never asked a man out. She much preferred being the one being pursued, instead of the pursuer.

But could she?

Well, why not? After all, she wasn't a blushing child anymore. She owned her own house, her own business. Why couldn't she take control of her social life and go after the things she wanted? Besides, Bea was right. She loved sharing her food. That's what gave her joy. And Jack had eaten a burger at lunch, the poor creature. His cholesterol was probably sky-high. He needed to know that good food could be healthy, too.

It didn't have to be her *pursuing* him. She'd simply be doing him a favor, giving him a good meal.

That didn't sound so bad.

"Hello? Earth to Mom?" She was stirred from her thoughts when Bea spoke again. "So?"

"I'll think about it," she mumbled. "Now. When do you come home?"

"Do *more* than think of it. Take action. Isn't that what you always told me?" she said firmly, as Valentina tried to remember why she'd raised a child who remembered her every word of advice, only to spit it right back at her later.

"When I said that, I was talking about your career! Your college major choice!"

"It applies to other things, too," she said, and Valentina could hear the smile in her voice. She didn't seem quite so tired now. "I'm coming back in a few days. Can't wait."

"All right. *Ciao, tesoro.*"

Valentina ended the call and stood there, in the kitchen, for a long time, thinking about Bea's words. Then she finished screwing the lids on her sauce jars, slipped them in the refrigerator, and went to her foyer mirror. She pushed a lock of hair back from her face, into her low ponytail, and checked to see if there was anything in her teeth.

"All right," she said aloud to her reflection as she reached for the door. "Fine. I'll show him who's boss."

She stepped out the door, climbed on her bicycle and pedaled down her driveway, to the main road.

Because the homes were spaced so generously apart, she only passed one of them on the way to Tom's apartments, the one Ellie lived in with her husband, a small log ranch that was always well maintained. Ellie's husband, Bob, was wrestling with a bag from his lawnmower as she sailed past, and waved at her. She waved back.

"Looks like it's gonna rain any minute now, Val!" he called to her, pointing at the sky. "Don't get yourself caught in it!"

She nodded her understanding and pedaled faster, glad that Tom's apartments were mostly hidden by trees and weren't visible by nosy neighbors, since Ellie was nearly as bad as Lola. As she coasted down the hill, she realized that there was a different car, a green Audi, parked in front.

Either Jack got a loaner, or Tom rented another apartment, she thought, braking in the dirt drive, sending dust into the air.

The apartment building wasn't very big; there were only four efficiency-style units, all on different sides of the square, one-story building. The two she saw from her vantage point had the window shades drawn tightly, so she assumed no one lived there. On the other side, by the barn-style garage, the shades were open, and a couple of windows were cracked an inch or so. One window was actually totally boarded up, which was rather suspicious. Had someone broken it? She hadn't noticed that before.

His bike was propped up near the door. She climbed off her bike and propped hers next to it.

Then she went to the door, took a deep breath, and rang the bell.

A moment later, it swung open to reveal a tanned, tall, platinum blonde, in a pale pink silk blouse and dangling earrings. She was professional, city-slick, her make-up applied to perfection. She stared through the screen door at Valentina for a moment, waiting for a sales pitch, maybe. After a few beats, she said, "Yes?"

Absolute humiliation threatened to creep over Valentina, like a veil. She tamped it down. "I'm sorry. I must have the wrong apartment. I was looking for Jack."

She started to back away, but the woman smiled through her pink-painted lips, her long coin earrings jingling as she nodded. "Oh, no. No, no! You have it right! He's right here."

She gritted her teeth as the woman looked back into the apartment and called Jack's name. *Remember. You're just offering food.*

The woman gave her an apologetic look. "Sorry. Looks like he just popped in the shower, actually. Can I help with anything?"

Valentina shook her head. "I didn't realize he had company. I came to . . ." *Ask him to dinner?* She couldn't say that. She didn't even know who this woman was. She frowned. "I'm sorry, I didn't realize Jack was staying here with anyone else?"

There was a slight rustling from within the apartment. "Someone at the door?" Jack called from behind her, and then suddenly he appeared, hair wet, in jeans, shirtless, but only for a blink. He pulled a polo over his head and as his face came into view, his eyes caught on Valentina and widened.

Guilty.

The woman nodded. "Yes, I'm Erica, Jack's fiancé." She looked over at him, and Jack's jaw tightened as he tucked his shirt and averted Valentina's eyes. "Well, I'll let you catch up."

She disappeared, leaving Valentina wishing she could, too. Instead, she stared at him. "I came to ask you to dinner," she said in a low voice. "But it seems that you are otherwise occupied."

"Valentina. I can explain," he started, sheepish.

"No. It's not necessary," she said firmly, taking a step back even as he took one closer.

Bea was right. Valentina was in control of her life. The boss of it all. And she could decide who to keep in it, and who to cut out.

Chapter Fourteen

Well, that's just great.

"Valentina! Wait!" Jack shouted, scuffing into his boots. He'd barely gotten them on when he heard her pedaling away on her bicycle. Tripping over the laces, he pushed open the screen door and shot out onto the stoop, only to see her flying down the street, disappearing out of view behind the tall trees.

He punched the door jamb and muttered a curse under his breath as he watched the dust, settling in the driveway.

Erica stood behind him, thumbing something into her phone, her red-painted thumbnails making a clicking noise on the glass display. She was beautiful, yes, the type most other women were probably envious of. *On the surface.* But get to know her, and she could be abrasive. Loud. A little bit too self-obsessed and materialistic. Opinionated, with a tendency to argue with anyone who didn't agree with her. Intensely competitive, against anyone willing to play. Whenever they went out for a few beers, she always wound up drinking too much and getting sloppy. How many times since college had he dragged her home and set her up in her bed with a bottle of water and a couple of aspirin? A dozen? She worked hard, played harder.

Yvonne had been a little jealous of Erica, once, too, until she'd gotten to know her and saw the cracks in her Miss America façade.

The mere thought that people could consider the two of them a couple? Not quite insulting, but . . . certainly a little demeaning. She was nice, and loyal, and sure, she'd make some man a great wife, one day, *if* the guy had the patience of a saint.

She looked up for a blink, practically oblivious. "Did I speak out of turn?"

His frown deepened. "You could say that."

Erica shrugged. "We did agree, if anyone asked, you were my fiancé. Just going by the script."

They had, actually, not fifteen minutes prior. But he hadn't expected the first person for her to see, right out of the gate, not an hour after arriving, to be Valentina. In fact, he'd kind of hoped he could've kept Erica and Valentina apart for the duration of her investigation. "Yes, but . . ."

She lifted her thickly made-up eyelashes to look at him. "Wait. Are you . . . and she . . .?" She pointed vaguely in the direction Valentina had sped off in, and her mouth opened to an O.

He simply shook his head and stomped back to the bathroom to finish the shave he'd been interrupted from.

"I'll take that as a yes!" she called.

Of course she would. Now, she'd probably spread it to all their mutual friends. It was always a big thing, whenever they went out for a few beers, whether Jack was "seeing anyone." She loved to egg him on about it. He'd always been glad to reply no, because he didn't need those complications.

He *still* didn't need those complications. He stuck his head out into the hallway. "It's a no."

"Then why are you pissed at me?" she asked with a sly smile in his direction. "The last thing I wanted to do was make things sticky for you. What is she . . . Spanish?"

He pulled off his shirt and lathered up his face in front of the bathroom mirror. This was probably a bad idea, having her come out. It was going to have his cover blown, and quick. They needed to get this wrapped up as quickly as possible. He rinsed his razor under the water, preparing to make the first swipe around his goatee, and said, "I don't know. I don't care."

"Well . . . you should date *someone*. Maybe then you'll stop moping around about that beast of an ex of yours. Don't you want to just get out there, to give Yvonne a big F U and show her you moved on?"

You effectively put a nail on the coffin of Valentina ever being that someone, he thought, swiping the razor down his cheek. And he might have been competitive with work, and with Erica, but he'd never been competitive with Yvonne. In that whole situation, he knew he was the big loser. Didn't matter how far he moved on; it meant he didn't get to see his kids.

Shit. Valentina had wanted to ask him to dinner. How sweet of her. Considering she'd hated him, the first time he met her, he'd made progress. And now, the boulder he'd been pushing up the hill had just rolled back down . . . right over him.

He needed to go to her house and talk to her. He couldn't leave things like this, with her, cursing his name and hating him forever.

Erica appeared in the door. "Don't you think?"

He glared at her reflection through the mirror and rinsed out his razor. "No. I think we should stop talking about this."

"Jack. It's been a while since Yvonne dumped you. You had every right to grieve. Every right to mourn the loss of your marriage. But you also need to realize that you should get back out there. You're too young to spend the rest of your life alone."

He shook his head. "I like alone. Besides, what about you? You're single, if I recall correctly. Perpetually?"

She made a disgusted face. "I'm dating here and there. But they're all bozos. Like you," she said, inspecting her fingernails. "When I find Chris Pratt, and he loves me enough to become a barefoot and pregnant stay-at-home dad, then I will be happy."

"Yeah. Not likely."

She leaned her head against the door jamb. "But you? You're easy-going. Fun. Simple to get along with. You don't have nearly as many hang-ups about a partner as I do. So I was just saying. Your lover girl probably makes a better dinner than I was going to recommend. I was thinking pizza. Any good pizza places here?"

He shrugged as he tilted his chin and swept the razor up his neck. Yes, Valentina probably did make a good meal. He got the feeling Valentina would've made him something incredible, which would've been a nice change from the dreary beer-and-Doritos meals he'd been scarfing down each night, as he did his unending and ungratifying research. But it wasn't just the food he wanted. More than that, he wanted her company.

"Probably not," he said, not looking forward to sitting around the dinner table with Erica. She'd probably drink all his beer, too, and then she'd get belligerent about whatever was on television, from the baseball game to the news. As far as he was concerned, the sooner he could get her to wrap up her part of this investigation, the better. "Have you found anything out?"

"No," she called to him as she walked the other room, her heels clicking on the hardwood. "Have you found anything out about the fraud?"

All his research had turned up very little about the actual bankruptcy case. It looked like Sam and Tina Wells were gone for good, with a good chunk of the development's money. Although he had gotten the name of Sam's ex-wife, down in Atlanta, who might provide some details as to the missing couple's whereabouts, he hadn't really uncovered anything at all. The drug shack was the most excitement he'd found, which was why he almost wished Erica was not so gung-ho on doing things all on her own. He'd have liked to play an assist. "I've got one lead on the fraud case I'll be checking out tomorrow."

"Well, I have to get back to Nashville tomorrow. So I think it's best if I just go over there now and check it out. You'll have to give me directions."

He rinsed his face, patted on a little aftershave, letting it cool his skin. "Hold on. I don't think you should go there alone."

She snorted and when she called to him, it sounded like her mouth was full of food. "What? You don't think I can handle myself? Need I remind you that I graduated first in my class from the academy?"

Yes, he knew that. Since she reminded him of that, almost every time they spoke. "Yeah, but—"

"It's just a bunch of small-town hicks up here, anyway. What are they going to do, run me out of the place with their pitchforks?" She laughed at her own joke.

He pulled his shirt on and went to see her in the living room, hunched over the coffee table, studying a map of Long Lakes. She'd already confiscated the left-over fried chicken he'd gotten at the general store and was planning to have for dinner. So they probably would have to have pizza. He pointed out the general location of the shack. "Right about here. If you follow this road off the main street, and keep following it to the left, you'll get there eventually. But it's pretty hidden. What are you going to do?"

She stripped the crispy skin off a drumstick, folded it in half, and stuck it into her mouth, licking her fingers. "Relax. I'm not going to run in, guns blazing. I'm just going to get some photos for the file. That's all. If it warrants more, I'll call in back-up."

He frowned. That still sounded dangerous. He hadn't liked it when Valentina went up there, but for Erica, it was worse. She had a tendency to get carried away, biting off more than she could chew.

"Listen, *pardner*," she said, sounding a lot like John Wayne as she smacked his shoulder, "I am a trained professional. You just stick with your bread and butter and look into what you're good at, and let me do the same. I wouldn't want you getting your hands dirty. Let the adults of this operation worry about the drug ring. Okay?"

The corners of his mouth tilted up in a smirk. "Whatever you say. Just be careful."

"Don't worry so much about me. I'm a big girl and can handle myself. So stay in your own lane," she said with a glower in his direction. "Besides, it'll give you more time to woo that Spanish lady of yours, because I know you want to."

"Italian," he said, almost without thinking it.

He realized his mistake when a smile broadened on her face. She laughed. "I knew it."

Chapter Fifteen

Later that afternoon, Valentina opened her mailbox to a special delivery from Michelle.

It was in one of her standard blue Pyrex dishes with the snap-on lids. Just enough for one person, with a bit left over for seconds. And a little envelope, part of Michelle's gingham-check blue stationery, which said, simply, *Valentina*, with a smiley face next to it.

Valentina smiled. It provided only a slight reprieve from the overwhelming sense of humiliation she'd felt, standing in front of Jack, earlier that day.

Her thoughts turned to her friend as she cradled the dish in the crook of her arm and went through a pile of mail that was mostly advertisements and housewares catalogues. She hadn't seen Michelle since that day at the stables, over a week ago, when she'd undoubtedly been acting strange. The old Michelle would've stalked her home, waiting for her to return from the ride, or at least called her immediately, to find out how things had gone on their "date". But Michelle had been completely MIA. Valentina had called, a couple of times, just to check in, but her friend's phone had gone directly to voicemail.

Taken all together, it was certainly strange.

Maybe Michelle was in trouble. Maybe it warranted more than a casual phone call. Maybe she should've asked her, point blank, if there was anything wrong. That was the American way, anyway. Direct, to-the-point, no beating around the bush.

Valentina scolded herself when she realized her mind had been so preoccupied with thoughts of Jack that she'd pushed her friend's absence to the backburner.

Stupidly, she thought, thinking of that woman. Erica. Confident and well put-together, she was clearly someone who took care of herself, the exact type of woman Valentina would picture on the arm of a man like Jack.

She cringed in the near ninety-degree weather as she reached for the front door. How idiotic she'd been, thinking he might actually have been a decent man.

The nerve of him! He'd clearly asked Valentina on a date. What was he doing, thinking he could play around while his fiancé was away? That poor woman. Did she even know what kind of man she was about to marry? Wasn't she even the least bit concerned when a strange woman showed up at her fiancé's front door?

Well, if one good thing came from that humiliating experience, maybe it would get poor Erica to question the nature of her relationship with Jack.

Valentina hoped she did. She hoped that right now, they were in the middle of the biggest argument of their lives. Jack deserved it. He deserved to answer to *someone* for his behavior.

Valentina closed the front door to the heat and leaned against it until long after the locking mechanism engaged, thinking. Dante and Luna sniffed at her, wanting to see what she held in her hands.

She nudged them away and navigated between them, holding the dish out of their reach.

Then looked at the dish and cursed herself. *I have good food. Good friends. A good life. I need nothing more. No more thinking of him. Wipe him from your mind.*

She strode purposefully to the kitchen, placed the plate on the counter, and opened the envelope, extracting the folded letter. Unfolding it, she read:

Valentina,

This recipe's from my mama's book. She used to make the best Country Captain. Not sure you like curry, but thought you'd want to give it a try! Just pop it in the micro for a minute!

Xo, M

Valentina pried open the lid, and even without sniffing, the overpowering, spicy-sweet scent of curry filled the room. She caught sight of a few almonds, golden raisins, onions, and chicken, floating in a brownish sauce, atop a bed of white rice.

Interesting. When it came to curry, she could take it or leave it, but today, she was definitely game for taking it. Especially now, since she wouldn't be making her *ciambotta* for anyone. She usually cooked to relieve stress, but now, all she wanted to do was . . . well, nothing.

She set the meal in the microwave for the prescribed amount of time and went to her walk-in pantry, where they had custom-built a rather large wine rack, taking up almost half the space in the room. She and Antonio were *oenophiles*, connoisseurs of fine wines, which was why he'd had the idea of creating their business. Truthfully, he'd liked the wine more than the meal; she'd always been more interested in finding the right accompaniment to bring out the flavor in her food. But it was the one thing that they both seemed to have in common, so that was why it made an ideal business venture for them.

She tapped her chin, thinking. Curry. A white wine would probably be best. The acidity and fruit flavor of a Zibibbo, definitely. Selecting a bottle, she took a plate from the cabinet and set it down just as her microwave beeped. She emptied the dish onto the plate, poured a glass of wine, and sat down at her place at the kitchen table, with the dogs lazing at her feet.

Being alone, now, she had nothing to distract her. She could really concentrate her taste buds on the meal.

She took a tentative taste and smiled. Different from what she usually ate, but in a good way. Delicious.

A sip of wine, letting the tastes combine and mingle on her tongue. Ah, yes. Delightful.

Still, as she looked around and listened, irritation crept in. The empty spots at the table seemed to stretch on forever. Because she had no near neighbors, she didn't have window treatments on many of the windows, and so the cold, desolate blackness of slowly descending nightfall seeped in. The ticking of the clock and the occasional beating of Dante's tail against the table leg were the only sounds, echoing hollowly through the house.

There was no denying it. She hated eating alone.

Being alone, actually.

Maybe something in her had changed, but she could've sworn she never minded it quite this much. In fact, when Antonio had gone back to Milan and she'd finally sent Bea off to college, she'd sat back on the couch with a glass of wine and *celebrated* the quiet.

Why was it so bothersome now?

She could call up Michelle for company. Michelle was likely alone, too.

Yes, that was a good idea. She *should* concentrate on her friendship. The least she could do was thank Michelle for the food. Just a few short weeks ago, that was her life. Food, work, home, Michelle. Simple, but she'd been happy.

Why was it no longer enough for her?

Ignoring that thought, she grabbed her phone and punched in the call. It went right to voicemail before she'd even lifted the phone to her ear. Again, odd. Until only recently, Michelle always answered on the first or second ring. She left a quick message of thanks and ended the call, now feeling more alone than ever.

She went to Antonio's old sound system in the living area, selected one of his classical CDs, and pressed play. The slow, lilting piano notes of Chopin's *Nocturne Op 9 No 2* filled the air. Back at her chair, she closed her eyes, sipped her wine, and listened.

Somehow, it only added to her desolation.

She drained her glass and went to pour another when the doorbell rang and the dogs went crazy, barking so sharply it reverberated against the walls. Settling them down, she headed to the door with them at her heels. She knew it was Jack from the shape of him, which she could see through the sidelight.

Apologizing, again. Was this going to be a weekly routine?

For a moment, she contemplated not opening it. She didn't want to hear more excuses. But then she saw him peering through the sidelight, directly at her. He tapped hopefully on the glass, a pleading look in his eyes.

Steeling herself, she pulled open the door. Before he could say anything, she held up a finger. "Before you apologize, I want you to know there is nothing you can say to change how I feel."

He nodded and crossed his arms. "And how do you feel?"

Did he not know? Wasn't it obvious? "How do you think? I feel betrayed. You didn't mention a fiancé. Had I known that, I would have certainly kept my distance," she explained fairly.

"She's not my fiancé."

Valentina paused, taken aback. She hadn't expected him to go down that road. She almost laughed. Of all the excuses he expected him to lay on her, that wasn't one of them. "Does she know that?"

"Yes . . . she does. Now."

Now? This was too much drama for her. She'd clearly misjudged Jack. She'd thought he was steady, honest, reliable. But this was so out of left field, and the second time he'd let her down. She didn't plan on there being a third. She rolled her eyes and went to close the door on him, but he held out a hand and stopped her.

"Look. I don't want to talk about Erica. I . . ." He stopped and listened. "Chopin."

Of course he was a man of culture. He probably had many other things in common with her, but she was no longer interested in finding out what. It'd only make the hurt worse. "Yes. You're interrupting my dinner. And I don't want to talk about Erica, either."

She could no longer close the door. He was still holding it open with his foot. She glared down at the offending appendage.

"Do you mind?"

"Valentina. Please. I don't want to lie to you. I just want you to know that it isn't what it seems. I did have a relationship in the past, and it worked out badly. I was hurt. And I don't want to hurt you. I had a talk with Erica. And she's going back to Nashville." His sentences were disjointed. He babbled, but he seemed sincere, or at least like he *wanted* to be sincere.

"I don't understand. Is she or is she not your fiancé?"

He shook his head. "Definitely not."

"But you were in a relationship with her?"

He pressed his lips together. "No. I mean, yes. We're friends. That's all. She grew up across the street from me. It's not like what you're thinking. It's not romantic. Not at all."

Valentina's brow furrowed. "And yet she thinks you two are engaged? Come on. I wasn't born yesterday."

"Val—"

"Let's get one thing straight, Jack. I don't play around with married men, or engaged men, or even men who are taken by another woman. She clearly thinks you're hers, so that's where I step out. I'm by no means anyone's side treat."

"I know. I know you're not. I never thought of you as that. And I'm not taken by her. I was married. I'm divorced. She got the wrong idea. That's all. But I've cleared it up. And tomorrow, she's going back to Nashville. That's all I can tell you." He looked up at the ceiling and heaved a big sigh, before meeting her eyes again. "I don't want to lie to you."

"Then don't," she said. "Why is that so hard?"

He let out an exasperated burst of laughter. "You have no idea. I'm really trying, Valentina. And I wanted you to know that I'd like nothing more than to have dinner with you."

She shook her head. "I'm sorry, Jack. That invitation has been rescinded."

He sucked on his teeth and backed away. "I get it. I understand. I'm sorry."

Valentina studied him. She could tell that there was something on his mind, something he desperately wanted to say, but for whatever reason, he was holding back. "You are very secretive."

He seemed to wither under her gaze, but he said nothing.

"What did you find in the woods? You haven't told me."

He was all too happy to tell her. "I wanted to. You were right. It's definitely suspicious. I think there's something going on. Drugs."

She blinked. "You think that Warren is making drugs?"

"Maybe. It looks that way. But you shouldn't get involved."

"Right. And neither should you. I hope you called the police." When he didn't answer, she closed the door, murmuring a "Good night, Jack."

Then she turned back to the kitchen table and her meal. When she sat down to eat, her food was already cold, and she didn't have the energy to put it back in the microwave.

It didn't matter, though. She'd lost her appetite.

Chapter Sixteen

Jack spent the rest of the evening thinking about only one thing: How he would make it up to Valentina.

True to form, Erica never came back to the apartment after her jaunt up to the shack in the mountains. Texts to her went unanswered, too. That wasn't unusual, since she usually got that way when she was following a hot lead. Everything else fell away. She'd packed up all her things before she left, saying she needed to get the heck out of Dodge before the place rubbed off on her too much. She was probably in Nashville again, or with the local police, getting things in motion to bring the meth lab down.

With that part of the case on its way to being tied up, it was now the perfect opportunity to work on figuring out where the hell Tina and Sam Wells had gone. He'd gone through text transcripts, company receipts, everything they had on file for Sam and his wife, and yet there was nothing. No records of them skipping town and taking a flight out of the country, either. They'd simply vanished, along with all the money they'd bilked out of Long Lakes' residents.

He had other ideas, other avenues to pursue, but his mind kept going to Valentina.

Late that night, after a couple of beers, Jack pushed away from his piles of information on the Wells case and threw his pen down. He wasn't getting anywhere, and probably wouldn't get anywhere, until he made things right with Valentina.

So he made a plan. Her lawn had looked a little long when he'd been there. Definitely in need of a trim. And he'd seen the Deere ride-on mower tucked under the overhang of the garage, before, which meant she likely did it herself.

She was a busy woman. She had her business. She'd probably appreciate the gesture.

Not that she was a woman easily bribed. He had a feeling he'd have to work to get back in her good graces, if he could even get there at all. Maybe he should've given it up, considered the whole thing lost, and moved on. Part of him wanted to. But the larger part of him, the one that wanted to get to know Valentina better, won out.

That was why, at nine in the morning, he cycled over to her house.

After last night, he knew that if he rang the doorbell and asked, she'd probably chase him off her property with a broom. So he planned not to give her the opportunity to say no. He checked her Deere, climbed on, and started it with ease.

He was about halfway through her front yard and two bags in when the door swung open. *Oh, here it comes,* he thought, bracing himself.

The second the screen door opened, the two big dogs came running toward him, as if shot from a cannon. He continued on his mission, riding in a straight line. Unaffected by the sound of the mower, the dogs ran wide, careful circles around him. He didn't look back at the porch, but he could sense her eyes on him. When he made a turn and came the other way, he had no choice but to look at her.

She was standing, arms crossed, mouth a straight line.

He laid off the gas and cut the engine. "Good morning," he said pleasantly.

She stepped out onto the lawn. Despite the early hour, she was fully dressed. He figured she was an early riser, and that he wouldn't wake her. She stood on the path and called, "What do you think you're doing?"

He shrugged. "Apologizing. Like I said."

She looked around, as if there was anyone around to hear them. But they were alone. Even so, she stepped onto the grass, and came up closer to him. "I don't need your help. Like *I* said."

"I know. I'm sure you'd probably do better without me. However," he said, wiping the perspiration from his forehead with the back of his hand, "I feel compelled to clear my name."

"And why is that, Jack?"

"Because you think I'm a scumbag, no matter what I do to try to show you otherwise. And your opinion of me matters. So I'm extending an olive branch."

Her eyes swept over the Deere. "By stealing my mower?"

"Borrowing. For lawn work. If you have any gardening, moving, raking, or what-have-you to add, please do. I'm yours all day, for whatever you need."

She raised an eyebrow. "Oh? Not writing today?" she asked, eyes narrowed.

She definitely had his number. He'd always known she was suspicious, but ever since Erica, she had every right to be even more so. He'd wanted to tell her everything, but he couldn't. Not yet, not when it could blow his and Erica's covers. But he didn't want to lie, either. Straddling that line with her last night had been exhausting. Not only that, it'd made him look crazy. Insane. And, yes . . . suspicious.

"Not today," he replied quietly.

Face still in a tight frown, she looked down at her sneakers, which were hopelessly lost in the overgrown grass. She shrugged. "I was going to do it tomorrow, after work. I suppose it needs it now. I'm surprised I haven't gotten a call from Lola." She threw up her hands. "Fine."

"Thank you." It was the first time he'd ever thanked a person for the privilege of mowing their lawn.

He went to start up the mower, wondering if she'd say more. But she didn't. Without another word, she spun on her heel and headed for the house.

The lawn was bigger than he was used to. The home he'd had with Yvonne had been one of those McMansions that she'd wanted, big on square-footage, with a postage-stamp yard, right next to the Joneses they'd had to struggle to keep up with. This was more his style. Spread out, lots of land. Smaller, rustic log cottage, but still a good size. Something with character. The house overlooked a lake, and the views were simply spectacular. More than once, he found himself pausing at the controls of the mower, just admiring the scenery.

Erica might have turned her nose up at this place, but Jack had to admit, it had a certain charm. He cut the mower engine and just listened. Nothing but insects, and a loon, calling mournfully across the wide, dark expanse of lake.

Yes, he could get used to this. One day, maybe he could retire here.

When he finished, as he was tossing away the clippings, he found a few overgrown bushes that needed trimming. He located at pair of pruning shears in the garage and set to shaping them. Then he got the hose from the side of the house and watered the parched flowers alongside the raised patio out back.

He liked this, making himself useful. Living in that shabby, two-room apartment for the last year, he hadn't had the opportunity to take care of things. He missed it. So even if Valentina told him to go to hell after this, it wasn't a wasted day.

But he really, really hoped she would give him a break.

Valentina was a neat person. She liked things a certain way. That much was clear from the tidy way she kept her house. He took utmost care in leaving things the way he found them. As he finished winding the hose, being careful to do it exactly as she'd done, he looked up to see her, standing in front of the sliding glass door. She was looking for him.

He made sure the valve on the water spicket was closed tight and jogged over to her, wiping the sweat from his face. It wasn't as hot today, but the exertion had made him sticky with sweat, dirt, and dried grass. "What do you think?"

She surveyed his handiwork and shrugged, unimpressed. "I made lunch, if you'd like."

An opening. "Yes, I would. Thanks."

He smiled at her, but she didn't return it. She simply turned and went inside. He followed, hovering in the doorway. "Am I okay to come in? I'm a little messy."

She shrugged and said nothing, just turned back to the kitchen.

Inside, he navigated between the eager dogs, sniffing. Notes of tomato sauce, onions, and fresh basil peppered the air. His mouth watered. "That smells damn good. What is it?"

She ladled something into two bowls. "It's my *ciambotta*. Vegetable stew." She brought it over and set it at the center peninsula, which was set for two. He climbed onto a stool at the nearest place setting as she pushed a basket of fresh-baked bread over to him. "You're going to send yourself to an early grave, eating all those burgers."

He nodded. No denying that. Yvonne wasn't much of a cook, but with her, he'd been a lot slimmer. Since the divorce, he'd put on at least fifteen pounds, mostly in the gut. Mostly from bad food choices. "I didn't have much of a choice. Too busy to cook."

"Ah. Well. Maybe I'll send you home with leftovers, if you like it. Give you energy for all that *writing* you're doing." Again, with the hint of suspicion. She motioned to it. "Taste. Let me know if it needs anything."

He averted her eyes and brought a spoonful of the stew to his mouth, pausing to blow on it. Then he sipped it. "Wow."

When he looked up, there was a hint of a proud smile on her face. No doubt, she'd made this dish before.

"You're an artist. This has got to be the best vegetable stew I've ever had," he said, grabbing for a piece of bread.

She let out a hmph. "Probably the only one, too, Burger Boy."

He laughed. She definitely had his number. "All right, all right. But it's damn good. I don't even miss that it's not a burger."

Now she had to smile. She sat down across from him and brought a spoonful to her own lips. She frowned when she tasted it.

"What? You don't like it?"

She reached for the pepper. "I don't know. I think I've made better."

Now, she was just showing off. He kept shoveling more and more of it into his mouth, not even minding that there was zucchini in it, which he never did care for. The potatoes, tomatoes, onions, and other vegetables melded with it so perfectly; he'd never tasted anything like it, even at some of the best restaurants in Nashville. When he got to the bottom of the bowl, she filled it again, without him having to ask. He finished that, quickly, too, and soaked up the sauce with the crusty bread.

"That was incredible. Thank you," he said, patting his full stomach.

He yawned and stretched, that familiar sense of lethargy creeping over him after hard work and a big meal. He went to grab the plate and help her wash, but she shook her head. "Sit. I'll take care of it."

He would've argued, but at that moment, all he wanted to do was fall over and sleep.

He scanned the area kitchen, the living room. He'd only seen her place from the door, before, but he'd been right. She was neat and minimalistic. There weren't a lot of knick-knacks on all the surfaces, and the mantle on the stone fireplace held only one thing—a portrait of a young woman in a cap and gown, a younger version of Valentina, with long raven hair and sparkling green eyes. He got up to take a closer look. "You have a daughter?"

She nodded from the sink. "Beatrice. She's nineteen, and in university."

"Really? Nineteen? You could pass for sisters."

She'd been clearing the plates. She looked up and let out a doubtful, "Ha."

"I'm serious." He backed away from the fireplace and admired one thing on the wall—an impressive display of hundreds of wine corks, each one tucked into a latticework that made for a striking piece of art. As he was gazing at them, some darkened by age, some fairly new, he noticed an acoustic guitar, tucked between an overstuffed leather chair and the hearth. He picked it up, then sat on the ottoman and started to strum an old song he'd known forever.

For a moment there, he simply strummed, his fingers moving idly over the strings. He'd played often in college, even had a terrible band with his buddies one year, when it was fashionable to do so. Never went anywhere, though. But it had always set his mind at ease. Gradually, as life had gotten busier, he'd abandoned his fun jam sessions. His old acoustic was probably somewhere in the garage of that McMansion.

After a while, he started to sing the words to the song, really, just a whisper. His voice had never been anything to write home about. But he couldn't hear the tune for this Bob Dylan song and not want to sing along.

When he stopped, he was vaguely aware the kitchen faucet had been shut off.

He looked up to see Valentina staring at him, her cheeks pink, her eyes wide with something like awe.

"How did you know? That's my favorite song," she whispered.

He smiled and strummed a little more of it. "Funny. It's mine, too."

Chapter Seventeen

Valentina took a deep breath as she checked her appearance in the foyer mirror. She could almost see her pulse skittering wildly in her throat.

He'd told her that since she provided lunch, it was only fair of him to reciprocate with dinner at his place. He'd laughed as he told her he wanted to prove to her that he wasn't some caveman who only ate fast food, for every meal. At the time, she'd been ecstatic. They'd bonded over their shared love of certain popular music, over their affection for the guitar, over their similar sordid past relationships. It'd felt almost like serendipity.

But now that the giddiness had worn off, she couldn't help feeling the full weight of that seed of doubt that had been planted in her gut. She did believe him that he and Erica weren't together, and that it had just been a misunderstanding on her part, but she couldn't fight the feeling that something was off. She just couldn't put her finger on what.

So when she slipped into her flowered blouse and long, flowing skirt, it was with a full understanding that if anything else seemed off tonight, she could easily put the brakes on things. After all, he was only reciprocating with dinner. That was all. That didn't mean there had to be dessert.

The heat and humidity from the past few days had broken with a late day thunderstorm, so it was a lovely night. The sun was just going down behind the lush trees, sparkling like diamonds over the lake as she set out. She walked, cradling the two bottles of wine in a sack in the crook of her arm, trying not to think of how nice Jack looked, his strong fingers moving over the strings as he strummed her favorite song. He even had a lovely voice. Plus, that song. It was almost like he'd reached into her mind and pulled it out. How else could he have known?

Shaking the thought off, she arrived at his apartment at a little after eight. When he opened the door, she noticed immediately that he'd put care into his appearance. He was wearing a plaid dress button-down and khaki pants, and his hair was still darkened and wet from a shower. The spice of his aftershave hit her, not overpowering and actually quite pleasant, as he opened the screen door to let her in.

She held up the wine. He took the bottles from her and set them down on the center island, allowing her time to look around. Tom really had let these places go to pot. They couldn't have been more than a decade old, and yet they were showing signs of wear. The furniture was cheap and mismatched, the appliances and other amenities builder's-grade. Ugly, garage sale paintings of woodland scenes hung upon the dark, rough-hewn log walls. A typical rental, she guessed, which explained the obvious lack of personality.

"It's nice," she said, inhaling. He had some food cooking, and to her surprise, it actually smelled rather good. "Oh. I brought a red and a white. I didn't know what you'd be having."

"Ah. Hot Chicken. Have you ever had it?"

She almost burst out laughing. Of course. She'd learned from her years in Tennessee that Hot Chicken—fried chicken smothered in brown sugar and hot sauce—was famous for clogging arteries all around the state. She couldn't fault him for his bad eating habits. It seemed to be a way of life around here. "No, I have not."

"Well, even if you have, you've never had it the way my mama made it," he said. "Low on the deep fry, low on the heat. So which wine goes best with that?"

"Probably the *Bonarda*."

"Okay. Well. It's almost ready. Make yourself at home."

She wandered around the living area while he busied himself in the kitchen. He didn't quite look at home there, but she couldn't fault him for that, either, since it wasn't his home. "Sure you don't need any—"

"Nope. You're my guest," he said, repeating what she'd told him, earlier.

In the living area, the small dining table had already been set for two. Though the plates were chipped, at least they matched. He set two wine goblets there as she scanned the rest of the place. Old, lumpy, flowered couch, outdated box television set, nothing very interesting. Nothing to shed much light on the mystery surrounding him. She motioned to the boarded window she'd seen earlier. "What happened there?"

"Oh. It was a break-in, a few days ago," he said nonchalantly.

Her eyes widened. "Really? Did you tell someone?"

He shook his head. "Didn't think I had to. Probably just some kids, after my loose change. Nothing was missing."

She gasped. "But if you'd surprised them, they could've—"

"They didn't," he said flatly, and she got the distinct feeling he wanted to change the subject.

Valentina fisted her hands on her hips. "Well, you could've told me. I would've double locked my doors."

Standing at the open refrigerator, he pressed his lips together, considering this. "I'm sorry. You're right. It really didn't occur to me that it was that big a deal. In my place in Nashville, break-ins aren't exactly rare."

"They are rare, here. As well as what you saw in the shack. You *did* call the police about that, didn't you?"

He nodded and closed the door. "It's being taken care of." He went over to her. "Hey, look at this."

He pointed to the top of the television set, where he'd kept the bottle caps for several different kinds of beer. She studied the display, wondering what was so special about it.

"You collect corks, I collect bottle caps. I'm so fancy," he said with a wink.

She laughed. "Very." She spun to take in the rest of the room. "Where do you do all your writing?"

He stiffened visibly, his eyes still fastened to the bottle cap display. "Hmm?"

"Your writing. I thought you'd have a nice desk, with your laptop?"

160

"Oh. Yes. Right. I've got my laptop in my bedroom. But I don't need much. I can do it pretty much anywhere."

"Ah," she said. "That must be nice."

"It is." He motioned to the table behind him. "I think the food's ready. Sit down. I'll bring it right out."

Other than Michelle's fine cooking, most Southern cuisine was far too rich for her palate. But unexpectedly, dinner was delicious, not overly spicy, and not dripping with the fat and calories Valentina did her best to avoid. He'd even provided a coleslaw which was surprisingly light and healthy.

"So are you surprised I know how to cook?" he asked, as he drained his glass of wine.

She started to nod, but he held up a hand, cutting her off.

"Don't be. This is just about the only meal I know how to make."

"It's delicious," she said, wiping her mouth with her napkin. "I don't think you are a lost cause. Maybe you just need the right cookbook to guide you."

"I'd say yes, if I enjoyed cooking. I might, if I had the time. I'm too busy, most of the time, to put much thought into it. A lot of times, I get so into my work that I skip meals." His eyes fell to his empty plate. "Barely saw the kids, missed a lot of milestones for them. I guess I was a shitty father. Yvonne used to have to force me to come home, sit down and eat."

"Yvonne is your ex-wife?"

He nodded, seeming surprised she didn't already know. He'd been so closed-up to her. It was the first time he'd truly opened up to her about anything. She could see he was being earnest. But something about his words nettled Valentina, and the reason suddenly struck her, all at once.

"Oh, right. You said this was your first book. What did you do before then?"

His eyes snapped to hers. "Nothing exciting. Just a regular office drudge. But I got over-involved in my work, trying to prove myself." He reached for the wine and poured himself another glass. "In some ways I don't blame Yvonne for straying. I was never around. But when I realized the error of my ways, when I tried to be there, it was too late. She'd already found someone else. And I had loved her but . . . she became someone else. Someone different from the person I married. A stranger. I guess I did, too."

She could see something in his countenance, regret mixed with shame. It tugged at her, and though she'd never spoken of it before to anyone, now, it just seemed natural. "Antonio left me for his research assistant at the office," she admitted.

Jack's brow arched in concern, urging her onward, but he said nothing.

Maybe it was her second glass of wine, or maybe it was because the room was dark, lit only by a single candle, or maybe it was the company. But whatever it was, she found that the second she started to speak about him, it all poured forth easily. "I was very young when I met him, just out of school, and he was a respected scientist, even then. I'd met the other woman, even had her over to my house, and silly me, I thought she was harmless. She wasn't particularly attractive, and she was a bit dowdy, to be honest. He was never one taken in by looks, but we had a solid marriage, or so I thought. I never thought he'd be interested." She stared into her wine glass before taking a sip. "But he'd been carrying on an affair with her for years, it turned out. He actually broke things off with her, and suggested the wine business to me, in effort to get away from her. But only a month into our move, he told me he couldn't live without her and insisted upon moving back, leaving me here, alone."

"Wow."

She nodded. "Bea had already been accepted to the university here, and I didn't want to disrupt her studies, so after the divorce, I stayed here with her." She finished what was left in her glass and laughed. "You know, I don't miss him. Not really at all. I miss the idea of him. But Antonio was, in a lot of ways, a bastard. I was too young to realize it when we married, but we had very little in common."

"I know what you mean. Things got better when I was on my own. But I miss my kids like hell. I miss having a wife, a partner. I'll be the first to admit I screwed things up. I know better, now."

They spent the rest of the time finishing the wine and talking about everything and anything. Before long, Valentina checked her watch and was surprised to find that it was after midnight. She shifted in her seat, then stood, more tired than tipsy. "It's getting late. I'd better go."

He stood up with her. "I didn't hear your truck. Did you walk?"

She nodded. "It's all right. It's nice out."

"And dark. And there's a bunch of thugs out there. I'll walk you back."

She would've argued, but the truth was, the news of possible thieves out in the Long Lakes community was more than a little concerning. One thing she'd liked about the development was that she didn't have to worry about her safety, as a single woman, alone. Funny how it hadn't bothered Jack enough for him to mention it before. "All right."

They walked back in relative silence. Many of the streetlights which lined the main road had not been replaced, so Valentina was surprised at just how dark it was. The only light was that of the moon and the stars. Jack, being the gentleman, took the spot nearest the traffic, but when a car drove past and forced them onto the dirt shoulder of the road, he grabbed her hand to make sure she didn't slip on the uneven path, and didn't let go.

Valentina almost laughed at what Bea would've thought, seeing her and this man, strolling together, hand in hand. Even she could barely believe it. She wasn't sure where things were headed, but there was one thing she knew. She liked him. And she was a grown adult, capable of making her own decisions. Did anything else really matter, as long as she enjoyed his company?

"So have you made a decision whether to consider staying for good?" she asked him after a while.

He shook his head. "I think, though, if I chose to stay, I'd pick a place on one of the lakes. Yours is incredible. That view."

She smiled. They'd reached her front door. She said, "If you haven't seen it in the moonlight, then you haven't seen it."

Though it was dark, she noticed his eyes widen by degrees as his lips twisted into a smile. "By all means, lead the way."

She opened the door, and led him through the house, out onto the patio, and across the back yard, to the long, narrow pier, disappearing into the dark water. The moon was only a sliver, tonight, and yet it cast an otherworldly glow upon the ripples of Firefly Lake. In the calm center of the black water, it was reflected in almost a mirror image, along with all the stars dancing around it. The only sound was that of their footsteps on the planks, the chirrup of crickets, and the resonant thrum of the bullfrogs.

They hovered together at the very edge of the pier, completely still.

"Yes," he said after a moment, now holding her hand in both of his. "This is even better."

A breeze tousled the trees. Instinctively, she raised her other hand to her neck, massaging the muscles there. He noticed. "Are you cold?"

"No." She wasn't even close. The anticipation was almost a living thing between them, so thick she could taste it. She gazed up into his eyes, and he met her own with an intensity that left her breathless. His eyes, shockingly light in the moon's glow, had such an interesting shape, slanted exotically, and yet thickly lashed, so intoxicating she probably could've stared into them all night long. Gotten lost in them.

"Tense?"

Yes. That was it. Her body thrummed with electricity, with something it hadn't felt in a long time. With need. Her every muscle was taut with it.

"Here," he murmured, dropping her hand and guiding her in front of his body so her back was to him. She trembled when he placed his hands on her shoulders, gently kneading the flesh through her blouse. "You are tense. Does that feel better?"

It felt more than that. It felt *glorious.* And not just because she'd been tense. The slow rhythm of his big hands seemed to work its magic deep within her, striking a chord that she'd nearly forgotten she had. She let out a little moan. She didn't want to speak and ruin this moment. All she wanted to do was concentrate on the feel of his hands on her body.

After a moment, his hands stopped moving, and he gently tugged her around so that she was facing him. She stepped closer, closer, and pressed against him so there was no mistaking what she proposed.

He dipped his head and kissed her as if something inside him had awakened. A long, shuddering breath escaped her mouth. They threaded arms as if that would stop the moment from slipping away. Her tongue responded with an urgency that she wasn't sure she'd ever felt before, in all of her life.

She broke the kiss, breathless, and whispered, "Let's go in."

Chapter Eighteen

Jack hadn't come to the house expecting to get lucky.

Oh, he'd wanted to. He just didn't think that Valentina wanted it nearly as much. Or even at all.

In fact, he'd been expecting to drop her off, possibly get a firm handshake and a thanks for the dinner. The most he was thinking he'd get would be a promise to see her again soon.

But the second he kissed her, he knew that he had been wrong. From the way she responded to his kiss, letting out a little sigh, her eyes darkening with desire, he realized she'd been thinking about this, about him, maybe just as much as he had.

"All right," he said in response, letting her lead the way.

She took his hand and led him to the patio, and in through the back of the house. The dogs made no noise from wherever they were as she guided him, in darkness, up the narrow staircase to the bedroom. She didn't turn on a light, but enough of the moon's glow poured through a skylight above, illuminating the white duvet on her bed.

"I have music," she said, and went to her dresser, where a slow piano melody began to play.

"Ah. This is perfect," he said with appreciation.

"Do you like Adele?"

"Of course."

There were other things in the room, but he didn't have time to focus on those. Didn't care. At that moment, she turned to him and gazed at him expectantly, without a word. He could nearly see her pulse, thrumming in her throat. She moved toward him and lifted a hand to his chin, running it over the cleft there. His breath hitched at her touch of her warm finger, caressing his face, smoothing the hair of his goatee.

"I like this," she said, tapping it with a mischievous glint in her eyes. "This dent in your chin. And the goatee. It's very handsome."

"Do you?" He'd had trouble believing she liked anything about him, considering she'd given him so many disgust-filled looks, since he met her. That was the thing about her that had turned her into his virtual obsession. She wasn't easy to please. He had to work for her approval. She was guarded. She never said what she was thinking. But now, she was laying her soul bare.

Trusting him.

If this was a game, then he'd won. But he didn't want it to be. No, this was more than a conquest, and he was determined to treat it as such. To take his time. "Do you dance?"

She nodded.

He took her hand gently and wrapped another around her waist, dragging her close to him. They moved, just barely, eyes fastened on one another, for what seemed like an eternity, and a heartbeat, all at once. "Valentina, I didn't come here to . . ."

"I know." She dragged a hand down to his chest and splayed it over his heart. "Just kiss me."

That was not a problem. The first kiss, out on the pier, had begged another. As if he were magnetically charged, everything inside him was screaming to pull her closer and do her bidding. He slipped a hand around her waist and even as he dipped his head, she lifted up on her toes and wrapped her arms around his neck, brushing her lips against his.

"This is nice," she whispered into his skin.

Yes, it was. That went without saying. His answer was to sweep his hand through her hair, drawing her closer so he could press his mouth onto hers. Their tongues and limbs tangled, first gently, then more urgently, her every tortured breath like music to his ears, her arms wrapping tight around him.

He let out a groan. Too good. She felt too good. And it had been too long. He'd wanted to control it, to take his time, but now he felt like a teenager, like he couldn't slow it down, even if he wanted to.

Her breath fanned his skin as she pulled away and let out a little sigh.

"Is everything all right?" he whispered.

"Yes," she whispered.

"Why did you call this place *Elsewhere*?"

She laughed a little. "Because I liked the way it sounded in English. And that is where people always look for happiness. But it's always right under their nose," she smiled. "And that's what I'm thinking . . . Just that I am happy."

A smile touched his lips. He had to admit that, for the first time in a long time, he was, too.

Chapter Nineteen

A few mornings later, Jack rolled out of the bed he'd shared with Valentina for more hours than was probably healthy, grinning from ear to ear.

Pulling on his jeans, he went to the picture window overlooking the lake, sparkling like diamonds in the bright morning sunshine. A thermometer outside showed the temperature as already a sultry eighty degrees.

He stretched his arms over his head and yawned, enjoying the feeling of the summer sun on his face. *I could get used to this,* he thought.

He *was* getting used to it. Almost too used to it, considering it'd only been half a week ago that he was pretty sure Valentina hated his guts. Now, as he turned back to her and watched her sleeping, her tanned body a stark contrast to the white sheets, her dark hair splayed over the pillow, he smiled wider. She had little freckles on her shoulders, a regal, swanlike neck, things he hadn't noticed fully until recently. The more he looked at her, the more gorgeous she became. Everything he saw about her only made him want to know more.

He realized it felt like he was falling into a deep pit, happily, with no desire to be pulled back up. All he wanted to do was keep going, in freefall.

She stirred then, blowing out a long sigh that made the hair veiling her face puff out. Wiping it back behind her cheek, she cracked an eye, and then groaned. "Morning already?"

He chuckled. "Yes. After eleven, actually, so nearly afternoon."

She groaned again as she flipped onto her back. "*Dio.* I have never slept this late in all my life. What are you doing to me?"

He loved it when she spoke Italian. It was sexy as hell. Whatever he'd been doing to her, she'd been doing it right back to him, and from the sleepy smile on her face, he could tell she reveled in it just as much as he did. He bent over her and kissed her cheek, sweeping her hair back behind her ear. "Sleep. You don't have to get up."

She pushed herself up and leaned herself against the padded headboard, the sheet pulled up over her breasts for modesty. "Oh, yes I do. I'm becoming lazy as a slug. That can't be good!"

He nodded, conceding his guilt, even though they hadn't been very lazy last night. Far from it.

Jack sat on the edge of the bed and threw on his jeans. He grabbed his t-shirt and socks from the floor. "I'll make the coffee. I'm going out to tackle the lawn. Wanted to do it before the hottest part of the day, but . . . *someone* kept me up late last night. Not naming names."

Valentina grabbed a pillow and launched it at him.

He caught it and set it down, then took one last look out the window. "You ever swim in that lake of yours? I might need to, after I get done."

She shook her head. "I'm not much for swimming. I don't even have a bathing suit."

"What does that mean? So it's just to look at?"

"I always talked about getting a boat. Just a little one. A rowboat."

"Eh. I guess you could, but how can you look at a lake like that on a day like this, and *not* think of swimming?" He winked. "Besides . . . you don't really *need* a bathing suit."

She wrinkled her nose. "Ha."

He shrugged and made his way down the narrow staircase, pulling his t-shirt over his head. The dogs, now used to his presence, perked up their ears as he approached, then jumped off their beds and ran to him, nails scrabbling on the wood floors as they rushed to be the first to greet him. He poured them bowlfuls of food, refreshed their water, and started the coffee, careful to do the tasks in the particular way Valentina liked to do it.

He poured his coffee into the travel mug he'd designated as "his" over the past few days and took a banana from the fruit bowl.

Outside, it was shaping up to be a scorcher. After lacing up his boots, he went around the back of the house, to the shed, and pulled out the Deere mower. As he did, he remembered he hadn't checked his phone since last night, when he'd come over for dinner. It was still in the pocket of his jeans—he hadn't pulled it out once, all night, which had to have been a record for him.

Now, he stood up on the mower to fetch it out of the pocket and stared at the display. Five missed calls, all from Nashville. Some from the general FBI office number, and one from his friend, Louie, who worked in his office.

Right. Work. Funny how he'd let it slip from his thinking so easily. The FBI had ruled his life for so long. Hell, even when he was a kid, he'd dreamed of being a fed. He'd killed it at Quantico, graduating first in his class. Becoming a federal agent had been the proudest day of his life. He'd given up dates with Yvonne, ultrasound appointments, hell, even a few Christmases with the family in order to follow some of the most time-consuming cases.

What had changed?

Valentina.

She was the reason. Something about her had altered the way he looked at things. Where before he felt compelled to prove himself as an agent, now he just wanted to prove himself to her. Maybe because she didn't know he was an agent. Didn't care. She liked him just fine for who he was, not for what kind of badge he wielded. Maybe he didn't want her to know.

But he'd have to tell her, eventually.

She'd be upset. Antonio had deceived her. The last thing she needed was more deception. She'd take it badly. It couldn't be avoided though. Though he'd worked hard not to lie to her, some lies were necessary. He'd do his best to explain and beg for forgiveness . . . when the time came.

He couldn't do it now. He had to get to the end of this case, first, or else risk blowing his cover.

Somewhere, in the back of his mind, he'd been making plans to continue his investigation of the Wells fraud case, but he always found reason to push it off until tomorrow. *Plenty of time,* he'd told himself. Or maybe he was dragging his feet because he knew, if he finished the case, he'd have to come clean to Valentina.

But it wasn't just that. He'd been running into dead ends all over the place. It was possible he'd have to say "screw it" and resign this folder to his growing file of unresolved cases. He'd planned to go down to Atlanta to have a talk with Sam Wells' ex-wife, but he hadn't been able to make contact with her. Not that he'd tried that hard.

Or, really, at all.

Even he had to admit, ever since he'd met Valentina, he'd been letting all of his responsibilities in Nashville slide, something he needed to rectify soon.

The guilt nagged at him while he mowed the side of the house, until finally, he decided he couldn't take it any longer. He cut the motor on the Deere and put in a call to Louie, thinking Louie would deal a softer blow than any of the other guys in the office.

Especially Dees. Bruce Dees, Special Agent in Charge and his supervisor, was probably spitting mad right now. He'd have to deal with him, later.

"Well, look who's been raised from the dead," Louie's strong Brooklyn accent came through. "You forget about us?"

"Haven't had much to report," Jack said, wiping the sweat from his brow.

"I'll say. Since you haven't filed a report in two weeks."

Shit. Had it been that long? He'd planned on getting his regular weekly report in tomorrow, but was sure he'd filed it last

Friday. Even when there was nothing to report, Dees liked to see whatever attempts he made in writing, just to confirm he wasn't slacking. Which he hated to admit, he was. "I'm working on it."

"Work harder. You're replacing me as number one on Dees' shit-list."

Jack frowned. Louie had always been kind of a screw-up, but he owned it, reveling in the fact that he was always one wrong move from being terminated. Jack had been the golden boy. He didn't want to be on anyone's shit-list, especially Dees', who never let anyone live any misstep down. "I'll give him a call and report in personally."

"I expected nothing less from you, man," his friend said. "We need you back in Nashville. Yesterday it was only Fiore and me. I can't take much more of that guy's bullshit."

Jack laughed. Brian Fiore was a blowhard, the type of guy who always had to do everyone one better. He, Brian, and Louie had gone through Quantico together, and when they started meeting regularly for beers on Thursday nights, he'd dragged in Erica, the black sheep DEA agent. It'd been the four of them, pretty steadily, for years. "Sorry. What, was Erica too busy?"

It suddenly hit him. It'd been a week since he last saw Erica. He'd called once, meant to call again to find out about the drug bust she was working on, but it'd slipped his mind. The hairs on the back of his neck stood up straight when Louie said, "Don't know. Haven't seen or heard from her. I called her a couple times. Went right to voicemail."

"That's strange."

"Not strange, knowing her. Nose to the grindstone."

Jack tapped his fingers on his thigh, thinking. "When was the last time you saw her?"

"Hell. I don't know. Weeks ago. But you know those DEA types. Always too busy for us."

Louie kept talking, about some golf outing he was planning for the fall, but Jack wasn't listening. He was thinking about Erica. He'd called her after she left Long Lakes, left a message. She hadn't returned his call, and like Louie said, that was Erica. But still . . .

Wait. The last time he spoke to Erica, she'd been heading to check out the shack in the woods. He hadn't spoken to her since then.

His blood chilled as a single thought consumed him. *Had* she left Long Lakes?

He spoke over his friend. "Hey, Louie? I've got to go. I'll catch up with you later."

"Yeah. All right. Get your ass back here soon."

"I will." He ended the call and quickly punched in another call, to Erica.

It went right to voicemail.

He pocketed his phone and spent the rest of the time, mowing and wondering what the hell had happened to her. Maybe he should've left a concerned voicemail message. Or a text. Erica was better at responding to texts.

He stopped along a fence and pulled out his phone, opened a message to Erica, and typed in: *Are you ok? Respond Immediately.*

Knowing Erica, she'd probably laugh at him for being so concerned. He stared at the message, willing the notification underneath the text bubble to go from "Delivered" to "Read."

It didn't happen.

Letting out a sigh, he put his phone back. *I'm overreacting. Erica's always been impossible to get ahold of. This isn't anything to be worried about.*

He was just about to throw the mower into gear when he noticed something. It was a small bump on the split-rail fence. He slipped from the mower's seat. At first, he thought it was just a giant insect, but as he got closer, he realized the casing was black, and a piece of glass glinted in the sunlight.

He stooped and inspected it more closely.

No doubt about it. It was a camera.

And its lens was pointed directly at the rear of Valentina's house.

He straightened, peering around, those hairs on his neck now prickling in the slight breeze. His eyes scanned the trees, the fence in the distance, the black lake, the pastures of sun-scalded yellow grass, all around him. Not a soul in sight, but he couldn't shake the feeling that he was being watched.

He reached down, grabbed the camera, and disconnected it, then dropped it on the ground and smashed it under the toe of his boot.

At that moment, Valentina appeared at the back of the house, in shorts and a tank top, her hair up in a ponytail. Smiling broadly, she waved at him, completely oblivious to the fact that she'd been under covert surveillance. He waved back, still dazed by the discovery, mind firing with question after question. Why was someone spying on her? Who? Was it a peeping Tom? Or something worse? Was she in danger?

But most of all, *What the hell was going on here?*

Chapter Twenty

Later that day, back at his house, Jack performed a thorough search of his apartment.

No tiny cameras or bugs. At least, none that he could find.

But if someone was watching Valentina, it stood to reason they were watching him. Which was why they'd broken in, a week ago. Maybe they'd wanted to plant a camera, then. Jack wasn't sure how much they'd seen. Maybe his cover had been blown. Maybe they knew exactly who he was.

Maybe that was why they were watching Valentina. Because of him.

And hell, if anything happened to her . . .

Finally, Jack popped himself a beer and hunched over his computer, rubbing the sunburned back of his neck.

He was worried that he'd been too short with Valentina. He hadn't told her about the camera, which he'd placed in pieces in his pocket, because he didn't want to involve her any more. And knowing her, she'd launch into an investigation on her own, which could only put her in more danger. He'd left her house shortly after finishing up the lawn, declining her invitation to lunch, saying he had to "work", a vague term so he wouldn't have to lie.

Now, looking at the pile of Doritos on the napkin beside his laptop, his "lunch", he realized he'd been spoiled by her.

But as much as he wanted to, he couldn't bury his head in the sand anymore.

She was in danger. They all were. He needed to keep his head down, stay away from her, and figure out what the hell was going on. And fast.

Jack stared at the cursor of his computer for a few moments. Warren was clearly into something bad with those drugs, and though Jack had done the typical, perfunctory search on him before and come up with no criminal record, now he needed to go deeper. Past the smiling pictures of him on his bank's website, past all the accolades he'd amassed as being Long Lakes' HOA president and Cookeville's star citizen. Thinking back to a conversation he'd had with Lola at the pool, he remembered a snipped of conversation.

His wife died. Hiking accident. Or so they say.

Lola clearly had a suspicious streak, but more often than not, there was a kernel of truth to those rumors.

He typed in *Warren Harvey wife.*

Immediately, a number of hits came back, all of them local news outlets. The headline: *Prominent banker's wife killed in freak Smokies hiking accident.*

Jack clicked on the first article, from the Cookeville *Herald-Citizen,* and read:

(Gatlinburg, TN) – Annie Harvey, wife of prominent Cookeville banker Warren Harvey, died from a fall during an early morning hike in the Great Smokey Mountains National Park yesterday, authorities confirmed.

The body of Annie Harvey, 43, was located approximately 100 ft beneath the Great Head Trail. Harvey, an inexperienced hiker, and her husband were on vacation at the park, celebrating their wedding anniversary.

"We've lived and loved together for over twenty years. I've lost my best friend," Warren Harvey said through tears.

Foul play is not suspected.

"The path was slippery due to an evening rain. Ms. Harvey was following her husband up the steep trail, and apparently slipped. This is nothing more than a tragic accident," Cookeville Police Captain Edward Briggs said. "Our thoughts and prayers go out to Annie's family at this difficult time."

Next to the article was the picture of a younger Warren Harvey with a slightly overweight woman with glasses and a short, dark bob. Aside from a bright, wide smile, she was otherwise unremarkable. Not unattractive but not beautiful, either. A woman who'd dedicated her life to caring for her husband and raising a family.

Jack sat back, remembering the man he'd met in front of his house. He didn't know him well, but Warren Harvey hadn't seemed like the cheerful, diplomatic businessman. He hadn't exactly seemed like a hopeless romantic, the kind of guy who'd surprise his bride with an anniversary trip, either. In fact, he'd been a bit of a jerk, the type who used his money and his big truck and fancy toys to impress people. Not to mention the shady drug business he was carrying out in the woods.

The man definitely had his skeletons, secrets that the rest of Cookeville and Long Lakes clearly didn't know anything about.

And something about that picture of the two Harveys, smiling together, just seemed false. Wrong. *Off.*

He scarfed down the rest of his lunch, took a swig of beer, and looked at his phone. Still no call or text from Erica.

This was definitely a problem.

He punched in a call back to Nashville, to Leila, the office admin. Leila was Filipino, well past retirement age but full of vigor, the unofficial mother to all of the agents. If anyone could be said to live for her job, it was Leila. The work was her passion. Despite having dozens of pictures of her grandchildren scattered about her cubicle, she always believed her retirement would cause the building itself to collapse, a belief also maintained by Jack and most of the other agents. The woman ran the place like clockwork.

"Jack Erikson! Well, hello, Bub," she said in her typically bubbly voice. "You have been missing me."

"Hi, Leila. Yes, of course. So I heard from Louie that Dees has it in for me?"

"You?" She laughed. "Oh, please. Never. Besides, you know me. I cover for you."

He smiled. "Thanks."

"You? I cover for. You miss a report once in a blue moon. Louie, he's beyond help. So how are things over there?"

"It's slow going, but it's going," he said, still staring at that haunting picture of the Harvey couple. "Listen. You think you can get me some more details about a case that happened around here about a year or two ago?"

"That's what I live for, Bub. I'm ready when you are."

"Okay. Her name's Annie Harvey. She was killed in a hiking accident in the Smokies."

She paused, repeating the name back to him as she wrote it down. "And you don't think it's an accident? I can probably get you the police report."

"Yeah. Great. And anything else you can get on Warren Harvey."

"Got it, boss. Doing it right now." A pause. "Police report coming over right now. And I'll ping you with anything else I find. Okay?"

"You're the best."

"Take care, Bub. And come back to us soon, okay?"

"I will."

He hung up, feeling a little better about the Dees situation, but that only lasted until he opened the police report. He scanned it greedily, which unfortunately took the lesser part of ten seconds. It mentioned that Annie Harvey had injuries consistent with a fall and that there was no sign of struggle. But it was pretty sparse. There was no interview with Warren, no diagram of the scene, in fact, an autopsy hadn't even been done. It seemed like the police's investigation of the accident had been heavily colored by Warren Harvey's brief account of the ordeal, since Warren Harvey was an upstanding member of society, and he'd been devastated by the accident.

Jack couldn't help but smell the bullshit. But he didn't know where else to turn, except straight to the source.

Warren.

He slipped his wallet into his back pocket and grabbed his keys, but as he was heading out, someone rapped on his door. He opened it to find Valentina, standing on his stoop with a casserole dish. "I thought you could use some brain food to help power you through your novel?"

He smiled, in spite of the nasty business he was dealing with, in spite of the fact that there was no novel. "Thanks."

He went to take it from her, but her brow wrinkled. "Something wrong?"

Maybe he'd been wrong to keep it from her. She already suspected Warren was into some bad things. And *someone* had targeted her, putting a camera on her. Maybe she needed to know what she was dealing with, so she would know to be extra vigilant.

He nodded and brought her inside, scanning the woods outside the house as he closed the door behind her.

He realized too late that he'd left his computer on, but as she walked in, the screen went to sleep, turning black. He wasn't sure if she saw the police report on it, but she appeared to be heading for the kitchenette. She placed the dish on the counter. "I made you *manicotti*. Is there a problem with your book? Writer's block?"

In answer, he held out the pieces of the smashed camera. "I found this on your back fence."

She inspected them carefully. "What is it?"

"It's a camera. Someone's been spying on you."

Her jaw fell. "My back fence? Are you sure? It might be one of those—"

"No. It's a spy camera. A little one. And it was trained right on your house."

Her eyes flashed with understanding. "Jerry. Jerry Vinton." She said it so definitively, Jack was shocked.

"Who? You mean, the guy from the stables?" The guy was a bit creepy, a bit squirrely. Honestly, Jack wouldn't have put it past him to be a pervert. But was there more? He couldn't help thinking of what Lola had said. *The Vintons are spies.*

She nodded. "Yes. He's the one I saw at the shack in the woods. With Warren. And a few weeks ago, Michelle and I saw him outside. He said he was fixing the fence. I thought it was a silly excuse. It didn't seem like him. But I didn't think he was a peeping Tom."

Jack scratched his chin. "It might be worse than that."

"What do you mean?"

"I don't know. What do you know about Warren Harvey's wife?"

Valentina thought for a moment. "Well, very little. She seemed nice. Devoted to Warren. When she died, we were all very sad. And . . . I do remember, before she left on that trip, the last time I saw her, she was acting very strange."

"How so?"

"Distracted. I was at the general store, and she was there, too, picking up things for her trip. She usually gave everyone a big hug. She was very friendly and outgoing. But that day, she was quiet. I thought she just had a lot on her mind, with the trip coming up. Afterwards, it did make me wonder . . ."

"About the rumors that Warren might have had something to do with it?"

Valentina shrugged. "I hate to say it. I don't gossip. But it did seem odd, because he and Tina Wells were very close. People said they saw his car in her driveway when Sam wasn't home. There was talk of an affair."

Jack frowned. "So we've got Warren, and Jerry, and Annie . . . Anyone else you know, behaving strange?"

Valentina bit on her lip, like there was something she didn't want to say. "My friend Michelle. From down the street."

He raised an eyebrow. "What about her?"

"I hate to say it," she finally said after a long moment's hesitation. "She's been very quiet lately. Doesn't come around as much. Something's not right. She's my best friend, and I'm worried about her. I agree, something's going on around here. But she's a good person. I can't imagine she's involved in any of this."

"Michelle . . . she lives in that cabin down the block from yours? Across the street?" He headed for the door. "I should just go and have a talk with Jerry. I'll stop by Michelle's after, then come see you."

She nodded and followed on his heels. "No need. I'll come with you."

He whirled to her. "No. Look, I know Michelle's your friend, but something's going on, and if it involves drugs and all these people, it's pretty big. You don't know what these people can do."

"You think it's bad?"

"I don't know. But until we find out, we shouldn't take chances."

She crossed her arms, visibly shivering. "But what about you? Didn't you call the police?"

"No. I said I was handling it. I didn't want to get anyone in trouble unless I knew for sure."

"But—"

"Don't worry. I'm not going to do anything stupid. And I can handle myself."

She returned a doubtful look, but relented. She followed him outside and grabbed her bicycle, straddling it. "I'm going to go home and block up all my windows, I guess. Please call me as soon as you learn anything."

"I will." He wanted to lean in for a kiss but she was clearly preoccupied by the information. She pedaled away before he could try, or before he could warn her to be careful.

At least he had leads now.

He went back inside and powered off his computer, then took his bike and headed out to the stables. When he got there, the stable doors were closed. He peered inside the office and knocked on the door to the upstairs apartment, but nobody answered.

Giving up, he pedaled back the way he came and headed toward Michelle's house. When he passed Valentina's cabin, sure enough, she had whatever curtains or blinds on the windows closed up tight, as if she were on vacation. *She better sit tight and wait for me,* he thought. *Last thing I need is to worry about her, too.*

Michelle's home was smaller than Valentina's, though much the same style. The wooden logs were showing signs of disrepair, so it looked as though it was a few years older. She had a large garden that took up almost one whole side of the house, with a *Welcome to the Cabin!* flag billowing from a pole on the front porch.

Despite that, the place didn't look all that welcoming. Michelle had gotten no such warnings about possible Peeping Toms, or Peeping Jerry, as this case went, and yet her windows were all closed up, shades pulled tightly. In fact, when Jack approached the front door and knocked, he thought for sure that no one would answer.

But the woman, Michelle, did, a few moments later, wiping her hands on a dishrag. She was an older, heavy-set woman with a doughy, kind face, but as Valentina had said, her eyes seemed cautious, and rimmed with red. "Yes?" she asked.

"Michelle? I'm Jack Erikson," he started, making a conscious effort to keep Valentina out of it. "I'm renting in the area and looking into possibly buying."

Instead of softening, her eyes narrowed. She seemed annoyed, like he'd bothered her. "And how can I help you, Mr. Erikson?"

"Well . . . I'm sorry. Did I catch you in the middle of something?"

"No . . . I was cooking. Cleaning up the kitchen. I left a mess." Her voice seemed softer, but still not friendly, and she didn't make any motion to invite him in. She stared at him expectantly.

"Before I buy, I was hoping you could clear something up for me. I heard through the rumor mill about some potentially illegal activities that might be happening in the neighborhood . . . and I thought I would ask you if you know—"

"Illegal?" She stared at him, indignant. "What do you mean? What kind of things?"

"You know. All kinds. Stealing. Drugs. I was hoping you'd know," he said vaguely.

She rolled her eyes. "I don't know anything about any drugs." She crossed her arms and her words came out like bullets. "If you're worried about crime, why don't you ask Warren? I swear I drove past his place and saw him loading a shovel, bleach, and a plastic tarp into his pick-up. If that isn't suspicious, I don't know what is."

Jack just stared. A shovel? Bleach? A plastic tarp? Sickness swam in his stomach. "Wait . . . when was this?"

"Two days ago," she said tersely. "Now, if you'll excuse me . . ."

Before he could ask any more of the dozens of follow-up questions in his head, she slammed the door in his face.

Well, Valentina, that's a really nice friend you have.

But he'd heard enough to know that nothing about this case was what it seemed.

Maybe Michelle was just trying to throw him off her scent. Or maybe not. Because with that list of items, it sure sounded like Warren Harvey was trying to conceal a body.

Whose body?

The thought came to him in a rush.

Shit.

He turned to leave, then spied the window. The blind was tilted slightly, a single eye peering back at him.

He dashed back to his bicycle and pedaled off in a hurry. He passed Valentina's house, deciding that he'd stop by later. The afternoon light was quickly dissolving to dusk, and he couldn't wait. Not if the suspicion that was currently tangling his gut turned out to be true.

Sweat beaded on his brow as he pedaled without braking, going on memory to get himself back to that shack in the woods. This time, it wasn't hard to find. All he had to do was follow the tire tracks that had been left in the mud from the last rain.

Cresting the hill, the rusted metal roof of the shack came into view. He slowed only then, to make sure there were no cars parked outside. When he determined the place was deserted, he pedaled the rest of the way in a rush, threw the bike on the ground, and headed to the door.

He tried to twist the knob. Locked.

Whirling around, he vised his head in his hands. Shit. If anything had happened to Erica, and he'd gone *days* without knowing it when he could've helped her . . . he'd never forgive himself.

Stepping from the rotting wood stoop, he walked through dried leaves to the side of the house, peering in windows, as he'd done before. This time, though, all the windows were closed tight. His eyes trailed to the ground, where he noticed something among the tangle of overgrown vegetation clinging to the building's side. Just a small circle of black.

A hair tie.

He'd seen them before. When they were together, Yvonne went through them by the dozen, always losing them or leaving them somewhere around the house. But in the short time Erica had been at his apartment, she'd left three of them, in various places, one on the shower ledge, one on the bathroom counter, one at the kitchen table.

Without thinking, he lifted it up. His gut twisted as he noticed a strand of white-blonde hair attached to it.

Most of his work in the fraud department was in following paper trails, collecting hard copy evidence and files. That was why he'd left his Glock at home, unused, under his bed, in a small safe— though most FBI special agents were required to be armed at all times, his unit had no such requirement. He hadn't collected evidence for a crime of a violent nature since . . . well, ever.

Pulse quickening, he tucked the band in his shirt pocket and crunched through the leaves to the front of the house, trying to find more clues. That was when he saw it, on a rotten wooden plank that made up the front stoop. He crouched in front of it and ran the pad of his finger over the stain. Dried, dark brownish-red droplets.

Blood.

Suddenly, something crunched in the distance. An animal, likely. He looked up, and around, scanning the thick woods, closing the shed in almost night-like darkness, but saw nothing. As his gaze swept across the forest, something made him do a double-take.

His bicycle. Hadn't he left it right *there*?

He stood up, still scanning, intending to look closer. It had to be here, somewhere. He'd been frantic when he got here and had cast it off. It was just a matter of where . . .

Before he could take more than a few steps, though, he heard another sound, this time from behind him. The sound of footsteps.

Jack whirled to see the last thing he expected—a slight, attractive woman with russet hair, wound up in a messy bun at the back of her head. She stepped back with a gasp, almost more surprised from his sudden movement than he'd been to see her there.

She let out a nervous titter as he dropped his hand, which he suddenly realized he'd clenched and raised, for attack or defense, he wasn't sure. "Oh, you scared me."

"Same here. I didn't expect anyone." He relaxed. "What are you doing out here?"

"What is anyone else doing out here? Hiking." She answered carefully, her eyes darting around in a way that made him uneasy.

Her face was heavily made up, with thick, purplish red lipstick and heavily shellacked eyelashes, which seemed an odd choice for a hike. Valentina hardly wore any make-up, especially out here. Not to mention, she smelled heavily of perfume, and was wearing skimpy shorts, which wasn't ideal for the number of mosquitoes in these woods, but she did have on hiking boots, and big socks, which looked almost comical under her skinny legs. She *could've* been hiking, he supposed. "All the way out here? Are you from the development?"

"No. I'm from outside." Her words were clipped. She seemed eager to be on her way, which may just have been a result of the sun setting.

"You'd better get back, then. Sun's setting."

Her smile fell. "Don't worry about me." She eyed him curiously. "What are you doing here? You don't look like you're out for a hike."

"I wasn't . . . I took a bike ride out here and strangely enough, I lost my bike." He turned to motion toward the place he'd last seen it, scanning the quickly darkening forest once more. "But then I—"

He barely had time to think before something knocked against the base of his skull. A sharp, screaming pain reverberated in his head, and his vision went fuzzy, the ground rising up to meet him.

She'd hit him. As he fell to his knees among the leaves, he wished that he'd gone with his original instinct. *She's no hiker.*

Chapter Twenty-One

Valentina peered out the window for the thousandth time that hour, then closed the blinds.

The thought that someone had been watching her sent a shiver down her spine.

She didn't like being here, alone with that knowledge, during the day. But with night descending, she felt even more apprehensive. Even with the windows shut tight, dread pooled deep in her stomach.

And she couldn't stop worrying about Jack.

She thought she'd seen him on his way down the street, headed toward Michelle's house, pedaling fast and furious, a man on a mission. But that was hours ago. Surely, he'd have stopped by afterwards, if only to set her mind at ease.

Unless he'd found something.

Something bad.

A terrible thought struck her, then. Up until a few weeks ago, if asked about Michelle, Valentina would've told anyone she couldn't have hurt a fly. But now, she wasn't so sure. Michelle had been acting strangely. What if Michelle had, somehow . . .?

Ridiculous.

But that was just how her mind was working, these days. So many things around Long Lakes were *off*. And as much as she didn't want to believe it, Michelle was a part of it, somehow.

Valentina padded to the fridge and opened it, peering in. Not that she was hungry. In fact, with all that was going on, food was the last thing on her mind. She had the manicotti, there, a whole tray of it that she'd planned to share with Michelle. Next to it, in one of Michelle's Tupperware containers, a new dish.

Michelle had dropped it at Valentina's mailbox earlier that day, likely when she was out delivering her own dish to Jack. She lifted it off the shelf, opening the folded paper atop it, and reread the note: *A healthy Kentucky Hot Brown for you. My sister's recipe.—M*

Was it just her, or was the note too short? Too terse? Michelle was fond of using smiley faces and exclamation points to excess. But there was nothing of the sort in this note. She hadn't even addressed it to Valentina. It seemed cold, impersonal, not the outgoing Michelle she knew.

Maybe she'd never known Michelle well enough at all.

Valentina pried open the lid and inspected it closely. Not that she thought she'd be able to *see* the danger on the open-faced sandwich, with tomatoes and cheese atop it. In fact, it looked like all of Michelle's dishes—absolutely delicious. Sniffed. It smelled quite good, almost enough to give her an appetite.

But poisoned things probably smelled good, too. And yes, she was probably letting her imagination run away from her, but she couldn't help it. Not after everything she'd seen.

The dogs inserted their little wet noses into the space between her arms and the counter, trying to get close. They seemed interested in it. But they were interested in just about *any* food.

She couldn't take the risk.

Before she could think twice about it, she'd gone to the garbage can, stepped on the pedal, and scooped the entirety of the meal into the trash. The dogs stared at it greedily, but she nudged their snouts away and snapped the lid closed.

Then she placed the dish in the sink and filled it with soapy water as she watched night continue to descend. The sun was now behind the trees, casting the clouds in a dazzling pink that made it look like swaths of cotton candy. The shadows of the tall trees were growing long, swallowing her cabin. Soon, darkness would fall completely over Long Lakes.

She'd worry about cleaning the dish later. She was too worried about Jack, now.

She took her cell phone out of her pocket and looked at the display. No messages, except for one from Bea, telling her that she'd made her course selections for the Fall semester. Whereas normally she'd be thrilled to hear from Bea, she couldn't concentrate on that right now. She'd have to respond to it later.

Where was Jack? Hadn't he said he'd come by later? Or had she just made that up in her head because it was what she'd wanted to hear?

Jumpy and irritated, tapping her fingers impatiently on her thighs, she went to the window and tilted the blinds again. When she looked out, she already knew what she would find.

Nothing.

Letting out a big sigh, she turned to see the dogs staring at her, still looking sore after not being offered Michelle's food. They'd been following her all around the house, sensing her unease, waiting for the other shoe to drop.

"This is intolerable," she muttered, and it was made more so because she knew how to put her mind at ease. She'd just been procrastinating.

She grabbed her cell phone and punched in the call to Michelle.

For some reason, she expected the phone to go to voicemail, for Michelle to once again be so busy in whatever underhanded scheme she was cooking up to come to the phone. But it was more like the old Michelle—she answered on the first ring. "Hi, Valentina."

"Hi," she said, letting out a sigh of relief. Maybe she was overthinking things. "How are you? Thanks for the special delivery you left in my mailbox."

"Oh, you got it? That's my sister's recipe."

Was it Valentina's imagination, or was her voice clipped, tense? "Yes, you said that in the note." She hesitated. "I look forward to trying it."

There was a long pause. Finally, Michelle said, "Did you have something else?"

"Well, yes. I happened to be looking outside and noticed that Jack had headed over to your place? He said he was going to stop by here, and I was wondering—"

She stopped short when Michelle let out an audible click of the tongue.

"Jack," she said, her voice sour. "What is he, your new boyfriend?"

Valentina didn't quite know how to answer that. Yes, he was her boyfriend, if that's what they wanted to call it. That sounded so juvenile, though. But it didn't matter what they were. Michelle had never before used such a sarcastic tone. Hadn't they sat together at her kitchen counter, just weeks ago, and Michelle had gone on and on about how it would be a good thing if she got out and met a new man? Why was Michelle acting so absurdly odd?

"He's a friend of mine," she said bluntly. "Why?"

"Oh. Nothing. I just thought you had better taste in friends."

Valentina stood there, her mouth slightly open, shocked. So this was . . . jealousy? No, it sounded like more than that to her. Besides, Michelle was the first person to start disappearing on her. "You sound almost . . . bitter?"

"Not bitter. Just . . . how much do you know about that man, Valentina?"

She thought she'd known quite a lot, up until Michelle asked. Now, she felt like it was a trick question. "What do you mean?"

"I mean that he's been acting very suspiciously. Going all around the neighborhood, poking his nose where it doesn't belong. Asking questions. Nobody here actually believes he's a writer, trying to pen his new novel. We all think that's hogwash."

She froze. They did? "What people? And what do you think he is?"

"All of us think he could be DEA."

Valentina almost laughed at the ridiculousness of the suggestion. Then, a moment later, she bristled as thoughts invaded her head. Hadn't he been quite nosy when she first met him? Yes. Didn't he ask a lot of questions, but rarely talk about himself? Yes. Had he ever shown her any of the book he'd been writing? No.

But that didn't matter. He'd come from a place of hurt, and so had she. He'd been so sincere. He wouldn't lie to her about that.

"That's not possible," she said finally. "I'd know."

Michelle merely laughed.

Annoyed, Valentina snapped, "Anyway, I was just looking for him. Was he there or not?"

"Oh, he was here, all right. But he left hours ago."

Hours ago? She'd been checking the windows religiously, but was it possible she could've missed him? Or was she lying? "He did? Do you know where he was going?"

"I don't know. I don't care."

She sighed, exasperated. "Did he ask you anything?"

"All he ever did was *ask*. He asked me if I knew anything about any crime going on in the neighborhood."

"And?" Valentina picked at a jagged edge of her fingernail, shredding it nervously.

"Of course I don't."

"So that's what you told him?"

"Of course! What do you think? I'm a criminal?" Her voice had a hard edge. "Why is he coming around, investigating me, Valentina, if you aren't the one who put him on to me?"

"I didn't . . ."

"And Rob's a good kid. Yes, he had some bad times. He did things he's not proud of. But he promised me that's over. He's getting clean. He's . . ." Her voice cracked. "He's *trying*."

Valentina's heart flipped. It sounded like her friend was close to crying. "Rob?"

She inhaled sharply. "I know. We all want our kids to be perfect. And you have such a lovely daughter. But Rob . . . he ran into a bad patch a few years ago, and it's been a downward spiral since then. He's addicted. Meth."

Suddenly, the pieces clicked together, and the mystery surrounding her friend all made sense. Michelle had always been so proud of her only son. *Of course* she was acting distant, not wanting anyone to know what she was going through. "Oh, my god. I'm so sorry, Michelle."

"You don't know what it's like, not knowing if the next phone call you get will be from the police, telling you your child is gone. I live every day, waiting for that call. He's been in and out of rehab, lately, but now . . . I think we found a program that will help. He's doing so much better. But if he comes out, and that stuff is available to him . . . I'm afraid he'll relapse. It's just so *hard*."

"It must be," Valentina said, wishing she could be there in person to give her a hug. She instantly felt bad for doubting Michelle. For suspecting her. For tossing away her dish.

"And word is that his supplier is from the development."

Her jaw dropped. "From the development?"

"I thought it was Jerry. That day at the stable a couple weeks ago, when I saw you there? I was trying to find out if he was my son's dealer. But he wouldn't say," she sobbed quietly. "And it's been driving me so crazy. If he's ever going to come back to me and live a normal life, I need to make sure that those drugs stay away from him. But when Jack showed up, I thought he was going to arrest Rob. Rob dabbled in dealing himself, when he was desperate, but he wouldn't tell me who his supplier is, either."

Warren. It all made sense. The meth lab in the woods.

A sinking feeling tangled in Valentina's gut. "Please, Michelle. Can you tell me exactly what you told Jack? It's important. I think he might be in trouble."

"I told him if he's so concerned about crime maybe he should be looking into Warren. I saw him loading bleach, a tarp, and a shovel into his pick-up this morning."

Valentina blinked. "You did?"

"Mmm hmm."

It was exactly what she feared. Warren. The shed in the woods. If Jack suspected him, of course that was where he'd go.

And that meant she had to go, too.

"I'm sorry, Michelle, I have to go," she said, quickly ending the call and punching in a call to the stables.

"Hello?"

"Molly?" she asked, glad it wasn't Jerry. She grabbed her keys from the peg on the wall and hurried to her pick-up.

"Yes. Who is this?"

"It's Valentina," she said, turning the key in the ignition and backing her car out. The quickest way to the shed would be straight through the woods, on the horse trail from the stables. "I'm on my way over. Can you saddle up Sunny for me?"

Molly let out a laugh of disbelief. "Now?"

"Yes, now." She backed the truck fully out and switched gears, lurching forward.

Molly paused. "You're serious? But Valentina, it's getting dark. There's no way you'd—"

"Please. Just do it for me?"

There was hesitation in her voice. "All right. Right away."

Valentina ended the call and threw her phone on the passenger seat. She pumped hard on the gas, careening down the road, hardly bothering to pause at the stop sign.

Maybe he was DEA. Maybe he wasn't what he seemed to be. It didn't matter.

He was in trouble.

Now, more than ever, she could feel it. There was no time to lose.

Chapter Twenty-Two

Jack ran through darkness, leaves and branches scraping against his face and limbs as he stumbled and struggled to find his footing over the uneven ground.

None of this was familiar.

He had no idea where he was headed. Wading through dark foliage, one after another, he saw nothing through the black until it was inches from his face. His head throbbed, full of earsplitting pain. The sounds of his footsteps echoed hollowly in his ears, and the smell of decaying leaves clung to his nostrils.

He spun in a circle, trying to get his bearings, but it was all the same. Black. Nothing.

Daddy.

A voice cried out, sharp, fragile. Lily. She was in trouble. He whirled to find her, fanning his hands out in front of his body and desperately slicing his arms through the inky dark.

Suddenly, he saw her there, in the distance. An apparition.

He ran to her, reaching for her, but the moment he got closer, she ducked behind a tree and disappeared. All the while, her desolate sobs tore at his heart. He tried again, with the same result, stretching his arms out for her, his fingers barely touching her cornsilk blonde hair before she dashed out of his reach. "Lily. Stay," he breathed, exasperated.

No. You left us.

It didn't stop him from trying. Endlessly. He couldn't give up. Yet every step forward only took him two steps back. He felt as though he'd run a marathon, and yet Lily kept slipping from his embrace. Cold descended on him, and his breath puffed out in front of him in a white cloud. He licked his lips and tasted blood . . .

The pounding of the earth underneath him roused him from unconsciousness. He tore an eye open and realized that he was lying, face down, cheek pressed against the forest floor. The sound grew louder—it was the sound of tires, crunching through gravel.

The pain at the back of his skull was exquisite, sending red flashes and fireworks through his vision as he rolled himself over and tried to pull himself up to sitting. Everything inside him was on fire. Gritting his teeth and clutching his head with one hand, he managed it, but soon realized that blood was seeping through his fingers and matting his hair, melding with pieces of leaves and earth that had been his pillow during his fall. It was tacky and unpleasant, but he didn't think it was too bad—his skull seemed to be intact, at least.

Someone hit me. Who the hell had done that?

The woman. He vaguely remembered, through the screaming pain in his head, hearing her voice, high and frantic. *We have trouble. He was snooping, War. Are you coming?* It had sounded as though he was underwater, and she was a record being played at too slow a speed. Somehow, as darkness had descended, he'd broken into a run and escaped.

Wiping the bits of leaves and blood from his palm on the thigh of his jeans, he blinked and tried to focus. Whoever she was, she was gone now. He was alone.

But no . . . *was* he alone?

He'd heard the sound of tires before. Or was that just in his head?

He listened again. Now, only, bullfrogs thrumming, crickets chirruping, insects clicking and calling their normal nocturnal songs.

With effort, he twisted his body to the side to scan the area around him. The pain screamed through his head, jumbling every thought he tried to summon, but the dream hung heavy in his mind. Lily. He hadn't seen her in so long. He needed to call her and Brayden, even if Yvonne told him to get lost. He had to talk to them. When he got out of here.

If . . .

The thought of his kids was all the motivation he needed. Blinking hard through the hurt, he peered around the forest. The surroundings were almost exactly like his dream—he could see slightly ahead of himself, the trees in proximity, but then it all dissolved into absolute black. Above him, a full canopy of leaves, fully extinguishing the light of the moon. The shed—where was that?

An owl hooted above, followed by a distinctly more human sound, which seemed to quiet all the nature sounds around it. A shout. He listened closely, trying to snuff out the sound of his heartbeat, which seemed to pulsate in his ears, louder and louder. It didn't come again.

Again, it could've been all in his head.

That woman hadn't been in his head. Her voice was too engrained inside him to be a figment of his imagination. She'd been on the phone, talking to someone. Someone named War.

War. Warren.

Tina Wells. It had to be. Hadn't the rumor been that she and Warren had been carrying on an affair before she and her developer husband split town with all the development's money? So she was here. All this time, she'd been right under their noses.

Damn. I've been blind and stupid.

He reached into his pocket and pulled out his phone. Fingers cold and sticky with blood, they moved numbly over the display. No service, of course. The woman must've had a satellite phone. But he had his flashlight. He turned it on and swept it across the barren place, confirming the shed was nowhere nearby. The ground rose slightly ahead of him, and he could vaguely remember stumbling down an incline before collapsing. Several gashes and a cleared chute among the smooth leaf cover seemed to confirm that.

That meant they were probably looking for him. Thus, the sound of the car, the voices he heard. They were close, and if they did what he feared to Erica, they wouldn't stop until he was dead.

Shit.

He quickly fumbled to switch off the flashlight. The last thing he needed was for them to find him now.

He thought of Erica and his gut roiled. Hell. He'd sent her here, to them, alone. Sure, she was headstrong and wouldn't have it any other way, but he'd basically sent her to her death. There was no use rationalizing it. Michelle had seen Warren with bleach and a shovel, and based on the hair tie he'd found, Erica had been here.

And damned if he hadn't let her go off on her own nearly a goddamn week before he bothered to look into it.

At that, the guilt twisted inside him and his stomach rebelled. He leaned to the side, nose near the ground, emptying the contents of his stomach onto the earth. Dry-heaving, he wiped at his mouth and staggered to his feet, using the trunk of a tree for support.

As he rose, the dizziness threatened to overtake him. He saw the darkness in double, now, through a veil. Blinking in vain to clear his vision so he could see straight, he trudged, not sure if it was the ground that was uneven, or him. He found himself walking at an angle other than where he wanted to go, like a drunk, yet although his senses were misfiring, his brain was now completely clear.

Erica was dead. If he didn't find his way out of this forest, he would be, too.

He dragged his feet. They felt as though they were encased in cinderblocks, heavy and useless. He miscalculated and the toe of his boot caught on a branch or a rock, and he went down, flying over it. The world shook around him, but the resulting collision with the hard earth barely registered over the pain he was already feeling in his head. His ears felt as though they were stuffed with cotton, as the thud of his fall was almost soundless.

He tilted his head up to the sky and at that moment, a beam of moonlight filtered between the trees, casting its glow on his face.

He blinked, and things seemed much clearer.

Ahead, he saw it, cutting through the trees. A trail, much like the one Valentina had taken him on, during their ride.

That moment of time, laughing with Valentina while the two of them rode through the forest, seemed like ages ago, now. Jack let his head fall to the side as his mind gently pulled him toward unconsciousness again, to revel in that sweet memory rather than dwell in this excruciating pain, an act of self-preservation.

No. Jack blinked hard and jolted his head up. *Focus. Valentina doesn't take anything lying down. If you don't find a way out of here, Valentina will try to find out what happened. And she'll be next.*

That sick thought propelled his upper-body off the ground. He swayed, tottering to his feet, and followed the shaft of moonlight, stumbling and swishing through the leaves and undergrowth.

Suddenly the earth beneath his feet began to shake.

It wasn't until several seconds later, when he saw the silhouette of the rider, bathed in moonlight upon the trail, that he realized where the plodding vibrations were coming from.

A horse was galloping down the path toward him at breakneck pace, too fast, he thought, for such absolute darkness. Whoever it was, they knew these trails well. Jerry, maybe.

He dove from the trail without a second thought, rolling slightly on the earth before scuttling behind a tree. It was only when the horse came close that he recognized it, and the diminutive figure in the saddle.

Valentina.

He didn't have to ask why she was here. It was clear she'd come after him. But how the hell had she gotten all the way out here, in the dark? Was she crazy?

He jumped out from behind the tree and did the only thing he could. He shouted her name with the remainder of his strength, short but loud. Once again, nature quieted to the sound of the invading human voice.

For a second, he thought she wouldn't hear, but she pulled on the reins and her horse reared up, coming to a halt. The horse whinnied and stomped the ground, wanting to go forward, but she yanked the lead and pulled it toward where he stood at the edge of the trail.

"Jack!" Her voice was edged with concern. "What happened? Are you hurt? Let me call—oh! *Idiota.* I must've forgotten my phone in my truck."

It didn't matter. There wouldn't be a signal, likely. "No time to talk," he said, his voice weak as he reached for her saddle. "We have to get out of here."

Understanding, she shifted herself slightly forward on the saddle. Somehow, he summoned the energy to pull himself up behind her. As he did, she said, "I was so worried. I— oh, Jack. You're bleeding!"

She reached over to touch his head, but he pushed her hand away. "We'll talk about it more when we get back," Jack said, scanning the woods. Above, a bird screeched out a warning. He pointed down the trail and patted the horse's side. "Let's go."

She snapped the reins and tore off in an instant. The horse pounded the ground beneath them, through the darkness, undaunted. Clearly, it was familiar with this trail. Its rider was, too. How fortunate he was that she'd come along, that he'd been at this trail, at this exact time, considering the woods were so vast. Luck was on their side. He wasn't ready to relax, though. At home, when he could call back to the office and get some back-up on the case, *then,* maybe, he'd feel better.

Valentina kept digging her heels into the horse's side, her back tense and hunched, urging the horse on. With one sudden movement, though, she pulled the reins taught. The horse lurched and halted.

"What?" Jack asked.

She motioned with her chin. "I thought . . . I think there is someone on the trail. Up ahead."

He squinted. Blinked hard again, trying to see. His vision was still doubling. Only a small bit of moonlight dappled down from the canopy of leaves overhead.

Sure enough, there was someone—a substantial someone, from the looks of it, standing in the middle of the trail. "I think that's Warren!" she whispered.

He watched as the person soundlessly took a step forward.

"What should I do?" she asked him, breathless. "Should we try to talk to him?"

Jack had a mind for what he would do, if he'd been alone. He'd have barreled forward on the horse and taken his chances. But not with Valentina here.

Should he confront the man, try to talk some sense into him? No, this man was beyond sense. Erica was likely dead. And had he killed his wife, too? Probably. No, confrontation could get messy. That was for the agents on his force that actually armed themselves, who had experience in this kind of thing. He had to think of Valentina. He had to protect her at all costs.

"Off the trail," he said to her, his voice even. "That way."

He nudged her in the direction, but she shook her head. Just as the man on the trail pulled something out of his coat. Jack didn't see what it was, but he understood well enough when the figure extended his arms, leveling it right at them, and its silver surface glinted in the light. "But Jack, if we—"

"Now!" he barked, voice firm.

Before she could turn the horse toward the edge of the trail, a gunshot echoed through the night. The horse whinnied and rose up, jerking them backwards in the saddle. Pain exploded in Jack's chest as he plunged down, juddering against the ground with enormous and bone-breaking force.

Valentina, he thought, or maybe he screamed it, before he passed out.

Chapter Twenty-Three

At the sound of the gunshot, Sunny went insane, whinnying loudly and rearing up on her back legs.

Valentina tried to calm her, holding tight to the reins, but before she knew it, she felt Jack slipping from the saddle behind her, thudding to the ground with great force, and she realized the worst had happened.

"Jack!" she cried, slipping awkwardly from the saddle, her boots hitting the trail hard. The second they did, Sunny took off in a fever, galloping away from danger.

Bending over the heap that was Jack, lying on his side on the trail, she peered into darkness, in the direction of the gunshot. Just then, clouds must've drifted in front of the moon, because she could see absolutely *nothing*.

Someone nearby had shot at them. And he was *still* nearby.

She could barely get it through her head. *Warren wanted them dead.*

Desperately grabbing handfuls of Jack's shirt in both hands, she yanked him toward the edge of the trail, pulling him down the bank as fast as she could. As she did, she found his shirt gummy with warm blood, too much for it to be just a glancing blow. *Oh no.*

The sound of Sunny's retreating hoofbeats gave way to another sound—the slight rustle of leaves on the trail, footsteps, coming closer.

"Jack," she whispered, barely a breath, trying to see the injury in the blackness. It was no use. The only thing that gave her hope was, when she lifted her fingers to his neck, the steady throbbing of his pulse. "Jack?"

He let out a bit of a moan and seemed to rouse. "Jack, we have to go. Now. He'll find us if we stay here."

She managed to pull him to sitting, then wrapped an arm around him and with all her strength, hoisted him to his feet. But he was little more than dead weight. They stumbled together for a bit of time, Valentina her one free hand out to avoid the trees, but it was unbearable. She had no idea where to head, so she moved in what she thought was the general direction of the development.

She clipped a tree trunk with her elbow and a shattering pain drove up to her shoulder. She stifled the groan of agony that rose up in her throat. When she stopped, she heard nothing but the insects. It was too still, too quiet, and together, it felt like they were making too much noise, stumbling as they were. At this slow pace, they'd never get out.

The hopelessness gripped her almost at the same time that the toe of her boot caught on a protruding branch. She lost her balance and went flying forward, him toppling down behind her.

She wiped what she thought was a bead of sweat from her temple but was surprised to find her cheeks wet with tears. "Come on," she whispered, reaching for him again.

"No," he said, his voice gruff and weak. He sat himself up, only to drag his top half, with great pain and effort, to the base of a tree, propped in a sitting position. "No. Valentina. Listen to me."

At first, she didn't. She tried helplessly to get him into position to lift again, because she feared what he would say.

And when she finally gave up and admitted how useless this attempt was, he said exactly what she'd dreaded. "Leave me. I'll be fine. Go get help."

"I can't do that," she whispered, shaking her head fiercely.

She didn't dread the idea of roaming the darkness alone. She didn't dread the danger that might await her if she stumbled into the wrong people. The thing she hated most, she realized, was leaving him. In peril. Alone, when he needed her.

"Yeah you can. I'll hide here. In the dark, they won't find me. I'll be fine. It's the only way."

She kept shaking her head, sure that if she sat there a little longer, another option would present itself. She wasn't thinking clearly. She'd just been shot at. Her mind swam. She scrubbed her hands down her face, as if that would clear her thoughts. It didn't.

Just then, a branch broke somewhere in the distance, rocketing her back to reality.

Jack must've heard it, too because he groped for her hand and finally squeezed it tight. His was warm, but hers was like ice. He leaned down and brushed his lips upon the top of her head, then nudged her in the direction he wanted her to head. "Now. Go!"

In the next beat, she took off in a frenzy, hardly thinking. The only thing that seemed to rattle in her mind was that this wasn't happening. It couldn't be. How could a normal, ordinary person like her be out here, running through the dark? Running for her very *life*?

The first thing she did was nearly run face first into the branches of an evergreen. Tasting sap as the needles scraped her face, she shoved them away and ran, fanning her hands out to avoid future obstacles.

She fell at least a dozen times, tripping over branches and scratching her limbs on brambles. When she reached an incline, she was almost so out of breath that she wanted to fall down and sleep right there. But then she remembered Jack, and that spurred her on, renewing her strength. *Think, Valentina. This is not a nightmare. It* is *happening. Jack is depending on you. And if you don't get help soon, he could die.*

At the top of the incline, she reached the path she'd been on. She couldn't be entirely sure because of the darkness, but it seemed right. She and Jack hadn't travelled far from it at all. Pausing there to draw a mouthful of cool, evening air into her tired lungs, she searched up and down the trail, as little as she could see, for any sign of her pursuer.

Nothing.

Turning, she barreled down the path, as fast as she could, toward civilization.

Valentina had never been much of a runner, but she was in shape from her hiking and other activities. Still, running was not something she loved, and as she dashed through darkness, she remembered why. The explosion in her lungs was only rivaled by the throbbing pain in her calves and thighs. She had nearly run a mile, stopping only once or twice to catch her breath, when a stitch in her side gripped her. Doubling over, she squinted ahead and realized that the black line of trees gave way to blue velvet sky, blanketed in dark clouds.

The edge of the forest.

Renewed, she picked up her pace and burst out from among the trees. The windows of most of the homes in her vison were dark, but a few of them had porch or outdoor lamps, providing a small amount of light. *It has to be after ten by now. This place all but shuts down after sunset.*

From there, it was less than a quarter mile to the closest building, the stables. She saw the metal roof of the vast, squat building there, beside an old silo, stretching against the sky.

Her lone truck was parked in the lot beside it.

It was her best chance. Taking a deep breath, she began to run again.

When she got to the gate, she saw the outline of a creature pacing outside. It neighed softly as she approached. Sunny. Of course, she had the sense to come home. She stroked her nose briefly. "Good girl."

She rushed for the truck and pulled open the door, then fumbled around in the cup holders for her phone.

It was gone.

What had she done? *Had* she taken it with her, after all? Frantic, now, she felt the pockets of her jeans, her coat.

No phone.

Idiota. Did you drop it somewhere, Valentina?

She scanned the ground of the lot hopelessly, then looked up at the stables. A light glowed near the office. Someone was there, likely Molly or Jerry. Even if they weren't, there was a telephone in their office. And they lived upstairs. She could get help.

Just then, a voice said, "Valentina? Is that you?"

Valentina looked up to see Jerry, standing in the mouth of the barn, the light catching his pale, every-which-way hair, like he'd just woken up.

"Yes, Jerry. It's me." She began to tell him that Jack was in danger, but then caught her tongue. There was a good possibility he'd put that camera outside her house. Maybe he was just a small-town drug pusher, but maybe he was more. She couldn't trust him. Couldn't trust anyone. After all, she was pretty sure, as unbelievable as it seemed, that the HOA president and neighborhood's most trusted citizen had just *fired a gun at her.*

Calm, Valentina. Act calm.

She took Sunny's reins and led her inside. "Can I use your phone?"

"Uh. Yeah. Sure. Go ahead." He motioned her inside, to the office.

She handed Sunny off to him and hurried into the office, which was so small it could hold little more than a desk and a file cabinet, as well as a wall calendar with a picture of two pug puppies and a mug that said *I don't do Mondays*. There was nothing inside the place that alluded to Jerry and Molly Vinton's love affair with

218

methamphetamines. Picking up the receiver of the old-style phone, she quickly dialed 9-1-1.

The operator picked up at once. "9-1-1, what's your emergency?"

"I'm here at Long Lakes. A man has been shot and I think that —" She stopped when she had the distinct feeling that she was speaking to dead air. "Hello?"

She went to depress the switch hook button for the receiver to check the connection, but found another hand there, already holding it down.

She stiffened. And here she'd thought Jerry had been taking care of Sunny, in the back of the stable. Instead, he was standing behind her, much too close behind her, his awful, rotted teeth on full display in a rather wicked smile. The sour stench of his breath assaulted her nostrils.

"What are you doing, *Val*?" he sing-songed, amusement and malice mingling in his voice.

Valentina's eyes wandered. Sunny was still out, loose, near the doors to the barn. There was about six inches of space between the desk and Jerry's lanky body. If she could just squeeze past him and mount Sunny, she could escape.

She took the chance.

She broke for it, but almost immediately, his hands came down on her, grabbing her. Deceptively strong considering his lean, lanky frame, he clamped his arms around her in a hold that squeezed the breath out of her, dragging her out of the office, into the barn. He threw her on the ground on her hands and knees, and when she rolled onto her backside, preparing to scoot away from him, he grabbed a length of rope and held it up.

"You bitch. You really think I'm going to let you get away with this?"

She slid back against the wall of the barn, wooden splinters catching in her hair. "I don't—I just—" *Innocence. Feign innocence.* "What has gotten into you, Jerry? My friend is hurt. I don't know what's going on but we need an ambu—"

He advanced on her, ready to coil the rope around her and tie her up. "Your friend is a Fed, and a snitch. And he deserves to rot. So do you."

A Fed.

Jack is a Fed?

She was so caught up in that small piece of information that she barely saw the shadow that crept up behind Jerry. Certainly Jerry never did, not even when the shovel whistled down on the back of his head, sending him collapsing to the ground like a badly constructed house of cards.

Chapter Twenty-Four

Astonished, Valentina blinked away the starbursts in her vision as her savior ducked into the thin stream of light overhead.

It was Lola. She stared down at Jerry, a pinched look on her face, and shook her head slightly, her frosted curls bouncing. "I always knew something was wrong with that cretin, bless his black little heart. Black as his teeth, I'd say. The guy was never right in the head, if you ask me."

"Lola!" Valentina cried, tears mixing with her relief. Her body felt like a thousand-pound weight had been lifted off of it. "What are you doing here?"

Lola kicked Jerry's motionless body with a pointy-toed shoe, like it was a heap of garbage. "I told you, didn't I? My Buttercup's not doing so well. She knows she's going in for surgery tomorrow, and she's just skittish as anything! I came to cheer her up. Brought her some apples." She reached into the pocket of her sequin-studded denim jacket and pulled out an empty wrinkled baggy. "I think the more appropriate question is, what are *you* doing here? And in such a state, girl! You poor thing. It's all right now. You're safe. Lola's taken care of everything."

If only that were true. Still gripping the shovel like a weapon, as if she expected more attackers to spring on them from dark recesses of the barn, Lola reached out a hand to help her up. Shaking, adrenaline pumping through her bloodstream in a rush of heat, Valentina climbed to her feet. She scanned the area, looking for

Sunny. Her horse was no longer hovering near the barn doors. She hoped she hadn't run off again, sensing the danger.

Meanwhile, Lola crouched down and checked Jerry's pulse. She made a tsking noise. "Whoops. He'll be fine. Just catching up on his beauty sleep. I don't think I did any permanent damage. You know, there's a rumor around he's been dealing. I don't put it past him. Buttercup never really trusted him, either."

"*Grazie,*" Valentina said breathlessly, finding herself slipping more into her native language as her brain cycled through other, more important things. Mainly, Jack, lying there, dying in the darkness. Would he even be there when she got back? Would she even be able to find him? And what if he'd been hurt worse than Jerry . . . what if he was dead?

Her heart stuttered at the thought. She spotted a flashlight on a peg board near the office. She hurried over and grabbed it, checking to make sure it worked. After that, her mind spun. Was there anything else she needed?

This is crazy. There is no way to be prepared for this.

"So what were you two talking about?" Lola went on, following her toward the doors, expecting an explanation. This would probably give her enough gossip to keep her friends entertained for the next few weeks, at least. "Valentina? Aren't you going to tell me why I just gave our stable-master the headache of his life?"

Valentina turned back for only a second. "You saw. He was going to—"

"Yes, but *why?*" Lola fisted her hands on her hips, getting increasingly frustrated by Valentina's lack of response. "He might be a meth head but he didn't strike me as violent. Why was he trying to hog-tie you, again? Valentina!"

Valentina stopped.

"Look. I can't. Not now. Just . . . call *la polizia*. The police. Please. And get them to come out on the old dirt path . . . outside the development. You know the one?" Lola only gave a hit of recognition, but that was enough. Valentina paused, trying to visualize the directions. There was no easy way to explain it. The police would probably get lost, in this darkness, without ever having been there before. "Tell them someone's been shot in the woods."

"Shot!" Lola's eyes widened. "What?"

"When they get to the fork, tell them to go left. I'll try to be waiting there so I can lead them to him. I hope."

"Hope? What . . ." Lola, for once, was speechless, taking in the fear that was doubtlessly in Valentina's eyes. The seriousness of the situation seemed to seep in. "Valentina, you're not going to go out there, all alone, are you? It's pitch black! Especially if someone's shooting at people! Are you crazy?"

Valentina paused to take a breath. Yes, at that moment, she felt crazy. She still couldn't quite believe this was happening to her. Though she'd been trying to summon her courage, Jerry's attack still had her rattled. She needed to calm herself. She sucked in the chilly night air. "I have to go. He needs me."

"Who?"

"Hello?" A female voice called from outside, along with the creaking sound of footsteps on a staircase. "Who's there? Jerry?"

Valentina and Lola looked at one another. Recognition seemed to dawn on both of them at the same time. Lola said, "Molly," she said, giving Valentina a rather regretful look before realizing with alarm that she was still holding the shovel and quickly casting it into a nearby pile of hay. "Your hubby's had a bit of an accident, darlin'."

"Jack's in danger," she whispered to Lola, heading for the doors. At that moment, she didn't care if Lola spread rumors about them. Let them talk. That was the last thing on her mind.

At the barn entrance, she passed Molly, who was wearing sweatpants, her long, dishwater blonde hair disheveled, as if she'd just woken up.

"Where is h—" she stopped and gasped as she saw Jerry lying on the ground. She rushed to him. "What happened? Jerry! His head is bleeding."

"Imagine that," Lola said innocently, reaching into the pocket of her jacket again. This time, she pulled out a cell phone.

Molly groaned. "Stupid, drunken fool. Probably stumbled into a wall again."

Lola nodded. "Probably. Poor thing."

Valentina flashed Lola one more meaning-filled look before rushing out the doors. Good as ever, Sunny was standing outside, waiting patiently. She grabbed the horse's reins and lifted a foot into the stirrup, then snapped the reins, even before she'd settled into the saddle. Lola may have been a gossip, but she was a woman of action, too. Valentina had no doubt that she'd do as she was told.

Leaning forward in the saddle, she spurred Sunny on, racing against the still, cool night air, hoofbeats pounding the ground in time with her own heart. She had no idea what the next few moments would bring. Above, the clouds parted to reveal a sliver of moon, which lit up her path into the dark, foreboding forest, where for all she knew, a killer waited for her.

Chapter Twenty-Five

Jack woke to a dull but tolerable pain, just about everywhere.

Except in his shoulder.

No, his shoulder, in fact, hurt like a *mother*, so much that he almost couldn't bring his brain to remember what he'd done to it. Everything else paled in comparison. It felt like someone had taken a knife to all the musculature there and twisted it around recklessly. It was a stabbing, screaming pain that emanated and throbbed, all the way down to his elbow and his breastbone, up to his chin. His flannel shirt was damp all over with sweat, but it was positively soaked there, right near his collarbone.

He didn't have to open his eyes to know why. It was blood, and a lot of it.

It was actually a good thing that he just knew, that he didn't have to perform an inspection, since the pain was so bad that the thought of doing much else seemed absolutely impossible.

Warren. Warren shot me.

At once, it came to him. He remembered, quite clearly, the cold breath of mist, rising up off the trail as he rode behind Valentina, her dark hair whipping against his face. He remembered the gunshot that had ricocheted through the cold air, the pressure of the bullet, embedding itself in his body, throwing him back, making him lose his balance on the back of the horse. Then there was the weightless feeling of falling, knocking all the air out of him, only to crash to a sudden end when his body met the hard ground below. He hadn't had the time to brace himself, which was probably better. Loose muscles had less of a chance of sustaining serious injury.

Like the one in his shoulder.

During the fall, he'd landed on his good arm, not his head or his back, and in such a way that it'd cushioned him, rather than snapping. Sure, *that* pain had been a shock, but it had faded in time.

The stabbing in his shoulder? The numb, weightless tingling in his extremities, signaling he was likely losing too much blood? That was getting worse and worse by the second, making all the sensations in his body fade away.

He needed a doctor. Right away.

The rawness in his lungs, each time he dragged in a breath, was almost enough to choke him. He tried to swallow and found his throat was as dry as sandpaper. He tried to clear his throat, but could only get out a dull cough. There was some liquid in his lungs, and he wondered idly if it was blood. His heart thudded in his chest, but only lightly. Too lightly.

The last thing he remembered, he'd been sitting up against the tree in absolute darkness, waiting on a bed of leaves for Valentina to return with help. The leaves had rustled and an owl screeched overhead, but other than that, there'd been no sound after her retreating footsteps had died away. He must have lost consciousness, sometime afterwards . . .

The sound of frantic, nearby whispering stirred him from those thoughts, and he managed to tear open a swollen eyelid to the hazy glow of a camping lantern, propped in a nearby window. He realized at that moment that he was no longer in the forest. He was lying in the corner of a wooden shack, propped up not against a tree trunk but against one of the rough-hewn wood-planked walls. The acrid smell of bleach stung his nostrils as he spotted the underside of a table he'd seen before. He'd seen all of this before, and yet it was different. From this angle, he could already tell that the place had been cleaned out.

He was inside the meth shed.

From his place under the table, he could only see the bottom half of two people. Both were wearing hiking boots and jeans, yet from the size and the pink laces in the boots, one was clearly a woman. There was tension: She paced the dirt floor, and he fidgeted from side to side.

The voices were distant, muffled, as if they were speaking through woolen scarves, but he could just barely make out what they were saying. A man's voice: "I don't like it. I don't like any of th—"

"It doesn't matter what you *like*," a woman snapped. "We have to! He's seen too much."

"You're the one who knocked him out. A fucking FBI agent. Real smart."

"Stop. I didn't know he was—"

"Jerry told us. He told us something was wrong with that guy. He was in his house. He found his laptop with all that FBI stuff on it. All we needed to do was just sit back and deny everything, and--"

"I had to! He was here, snooping around. If I hadn't, that would've been the end of us. He'd be halfway to his FBI friends, telling them everything he'd seen."

"What did he see? We've cleaned the place out. He wouldn't have found anything. But now, thanks to this stunt, we're *fucked*."

"No, we're not. This is it, Sam. All we have to do is get rid of this one loose end, and we're free. All right?" Her voice was sweetly begging.

Sam. Tina. Jack had thought that female hiker looked suspicious. Of course, he'd seen her picture in the file. She'd looked different, though, in the photo. And here they were, the same couple that he'd come all this way to investigate. They'd been here all along. Running a meth ring, right under the development's nose, after bilking them of all their money.

A pause. "This is one *big* loose end. First that DEA agent. Now him? I don't know how you talked me into this. I said this was a bad deal to begin with. It's just getting messier and messier. You know if they catch us, we're never getting out of prison."

Yeah. That's right. They're in a lot of trouble, now. Stealing from the development? Making and distributing drugs? Evading the FBI? What else?

"That's why we need to make sure we don't get caught. Whatever it takes."

A loud sigh. "That murder was too much. Forget it. I'm done. I'm not doing any more of this."

Murder. Erica.

229

"Fine. Let War do it, then. He'll be back in a minute. He was always twice the man you were, anyway."

Warren. Shit.

"Twice the man. Really? Next thing you know, he'll be offing you."

"No. He did all this because he loves me. Because--"

"Because you know how to spend money like it's going out of style. Why do you think I got into the trouble with the development? Trying to afford shit for you and your expensive tastes. All those trips, those fancy dinners, those expensive handbags. After we split the money for this, we're done. I'm gone."

"Fine by me. Three ways."

"No. Half is mine, half is yours and Warren's."

She snorted. "We'll see what Warren has to say about that when he gets here. You don't deserve half. He's the one whose been covering our asses this time. You've always been too afraid to get your hands dirty."

The man's feet went toward the door, opening it, looking out. "*You* could do it. Get your hands a little dirty. Be my guest."

She didn't answer. Instead, she bent down to look at Jack. He pulled his eyes closed as she did, feigning unconsciousness. "That wound looks pretty bad. He might die on his own."

If it looks bad, just imagine how it feels, Jack thought, laughing inwardly to himself. He was vaguely aware that he was going crazy from the pain, losing his grip on reality.

Sam let out a bitter laugh. "On his own? Warren and his happy trigger finger shot him. Just like that girl. It's like you two think you're gangsters, or something. Ever since Annie, he's been scaring me. How easily he's willing to dispose of any obstacle in his way. And now you're getting the same way, too."

Hell. His wife, Annie. Two murders.

She turned and hoisted herself up onto the table, over Jack, so that her feet were hanging down over him. "Just calm down."

Sam closed the door. "He's taking too long. Something went wrong."

Jack opened his eyes again. His vision swam as he tried to focus. The pain and loss of blood was making him see spots in his line of sight. He blinked, again and again, and tried to reach up to feel his injury. Instead, he found his hands had been bound in front of him.

He could only hope that the something that had gone wrong was Valentina. That she'd gotten to the police somehow.

"Calm *down*, already," Tina repeated. "Stop being so jittery. He'll be here."

He closed his eyes. He didn't have the energy to open them again. Some time later, maybe moments, maybe hours, he heard the sound of the door creaking open, and heavy footsteps on the dirt floor. A tense voice, lower than Sam's, said, "She got away."

"What!" Tina shouted, hopping off the table. "Was it that Italian bitch?"

"Yeah."

Sam cursed under his breath. "That's just great. What do we do now?"

Inside, Jack smiled. *That a girl.* Maybe things were finally going his way. Maybe he'd get out of this, after all.

"We go on with the rest of the plan and get out of here. Quick as we can. Come on." Warren barked. "The police'll probably be here any minute. Bet she's calling them now."

"But what about the Fed?" Sam said, his voice full of indecision.

"Leave him."

The door opened. Jack heaved a sigh of relief. Now, he could get out, if he could just find the strength. He could make his way to the road, flag down the officers. He'd be all right. He just needed to —

He stopped when footsteps crunched toward him, and he heard the unmistakable sound of a cork being popped from a jug, and liquid, splashing out of it, onto the ground and walls around him.

The stench was unmistakable.

Gasoline.

Somewhere in his muddled mind spun the idea to fight, to jump to his feet and attack in one last-ditch hurrah, as hopeless as it was, considering his hands were bound. But his body simply wouldn't allow it. The most he could move were his eyelids, which now opened wide in horror. The door was wide open.

In the distance, he could've sworn he heard someone striking a match.

A brief moment of absolute clarity gripped Jack hard.

They're going to burn this place to the ground, he thought, as the liquid splashed from the table above, soaking his already blood-covered clothes. *And burn me alive while they're at it.*

He scrabbled to pull in his feet, to push his back against the wall, to stand. But his legs sprawled useless in front of him, still.

Three murders.

Chapter Twenty-Six

Valentina hunched over Sunny's neck and dug her heels into the horse's ribs. She snapped the reins, urging her faster as she galloped into the forest.

In the path, the place where she thought she'd left Jack, she pulled on the reins and peered out into the darkness. Ahead on the path, everything was still. Silent. No sign of Warren whatsoever.

"Jack!" she whispered hoarsely.

With the darkness had come a strong, bitter wind, rustling the leaves in the trees above. She listened, but only heard them in reply.

She tried again. "Jack!"

Nothing.

Slipping from her saddle, she left Sunny on the path and turned on the flashlight she'd gotten at the stable. She arced it around the forest in front of her as she descended a mild, leaf-covered slope, her boots slipping on the cover. She should've taken better notice of her surroundings, before, but she'd been too frantic. Now, as she shone her light on all the trees, she realized they all looked the same.

"Jack," she tried again, this time, her voice cracking.

His lack of response didn't tell her much. He might have fallen asleep. Or he might have decided to try to get out on his own. But hopelessness descended, weighing upon her like a heavy blanket. What if he'd succumbed to his injuries? What if Warren found him, and now he was dead?

She dipped the flashlight to the ground, until its sulfuric glow captured something that shouldn't have been there. Jogging up to it, she realized it was a cell phone.

Her cell phone.

She checked the display. Zero bars. Of course. This mountain was terribly spotty when it came to cell phone reception.

But she'd been here. So she was close.

Valentina swung the flashlight around until she noticed a spot where the leaves had been disturbed, at the base of a tree. She ran to it, falling to her knees. Was this the spot? If so, he wasn't here, now. She patted the leaf cover with her hands, looking for any indication that he'd once been here. Her fingers found something damp.

Raising them into the light, they were covered in blood.

This had to have been the place. But now he was gone.

She spun in a circle, shining the flashlight in all directions. Yes, definitely gone.

Breaking into a run, she found the path again, and Sunny, waiting patiently for her. Swift-moving clouds rolled over the moon, blocking out its light, and the wind howled in her ears. She climbed back into the saddle and, tucking the flashlight under her arm, snapped the reins, urging Sunny toward the main road.

She'd find the police there and lead them to the shed. And hopefully, somehow, she'd find Jack, too.

If only she could keep herself from shivering. She needed to stay calm. Despite the cool breeze, perspiration trickled down her ribcage. She rode fast, into a blur of leaves and swaying branches, the pounding of Sunny's hooves on the ground mimicking her own heartbeat. Adrenaline pumped through her veins, and her breaths came short and shallow.

When she came to the fork in the pathway, she took the right path, a wider path that was more of a straight shot toward the main road. It was less travelled, and not the one that she normally took with Sunny, but the other, the one that headed toward the shed, was narrow, balanced precariously on the edge of a steep drop and far too dangerous to attempt in the dark. This was the quickest way to head off the police.

Fragments of thoughts swarmed her head, half-baked plans that she wasn't sure were purely logical. She needed to get to the police. If Warren was at the shed—if he had Jack—she couldn't face him on her own. If Jack was there, maybe he was in trouble. Or worse.

She heard the sirens before she reached the main road.

Seconds later, red and blue lights, spinning, cut through the darkness, beyond the trees. A police car. Two.

Thank you, Lola, she thought, digging her heels into Sunny's sides and urging her to climb the embankment to the main road. When she did, blinking in their oncoming headlights, she took the flashlight and aimed its beam at the approaching police cruisers.

They slowed to a stop beside her, the sirens blaring until finally, mercifully, the officer cut them. He powered down his window. "We got a call of a shooting?"

"Yes," she said breathlessly. "I asked my friend to do that. A man was shot in the woods. I went to call for help and when I got back, he was gone. I think the man who shot him was Warren. Warren Harvey."

The officer had been intently listening, up to the point she mentioned his name. At that moment, he squinted in confusion. "Wait. Warren *Harvey*? The banker?"

"Yes."

Was it Valentina's imagination, or did he seem to doubt her, now? It made sense. She was a nobody, and Warren was Cookeville's star citizen. "And who are you?"

"Valentina Bianco. I live in the Long Lakes development. There's a shed up that way," she said, pointing her flashlight down the road, where it curved into the trees. "I think he was making drugs up there."

"Drugs? All right." The officer nodded and reached for his radio. "We'll go and check it out. Stay behind us, ma'am, but don't wander too far off. We may have questions."

She nodded and led Sunny back a few steps, so that they could proceed. They headed up the street at what felt like a snail's pace, too slowly for Valentina's liking. What if Jack was in trouble? Every second counted.

That was why, once the cruisers passed her, she led Sunny after them. Knowing Jack, he wouldn't run away from the trouble. He'd be close. Unless . . .

As the cruisers rounded a bend, their brake lights went on. The headlights of the first car illuminated a truck, parked in the very center of the dirt road. A shiny, black RAM with the Tennessee license plate: TITANS1.

Warren's car.

Beyond the windshield, Valentina could just make out that the cabin was empty.

Before she could scan the woods, one of the officers exploded out of his car.

"Police! Stop!" he shouted, into the woods. Drawing his gun, he aimed it into the darkness. Valentina swung the flashlight beam that way to reveal nothing more than a fast-moving, red blur, disappearing into the trees.

Two other officers popped out of the second car, grabbing ahold of their weapons and flashlights, illuminating the woods. "What did you see?"

The first officer pointed. "Over there. Let's go!"

The three officers tore into the woods without hesitation, leaving Valentina alone on the road with Sunny. She listened as their footsteps disappeared into the night, saw their lights, flashing among the trees. At once, someone shouted, "One went that way."

Two of them. Maybe more. Jerry was in on it. Warren. Who else?

Hopeless. Helpless. All she knew was that if it didn't come to an end right now, she'd be hunted next. Maybe she was being hunted, right now.

This wasn't safe.

She slipped from Sunny's saddle and led him down the path, now desperately wondering where Jack had gone off to. One thing was obvious. Warren wasn't the golden boy he pretended to be. He'd done some terrible things, getting involved with drugs. Annie was sensible; as his wife, she never would've put up with that. Maybe she'd tried to stop it, and he'd even killed poor Annie.

A sick feeling tangled in her gut. If Warren could kill his own wife, nothing would stop him from killing Jack.

She knew the officers had told her to stay behind the cruisers, but she couldn't help it. She led Sunny closer to the Dodge Ram, shining her flashlight in the windows, hoping for some clue as to where Jack had gone.

She laid a hand on the engine. Still warm. Both windows were wide open, so she approached the driver's side and peered in. The keys were still in the ignition, which made sense. He'd made a quick break for it. There was a Starbucks cup in the center console, and a cell phone with a pink case, its display lit up. On the lock screen, a photograph of a blonde, in a bikini, in front of a crystal blue Caribbean sea.

Tina Wells.

Back from the dead. But obviously, she hadn't gone far. She was in on it, too. Was Sam? Was everyone at Long Lakes involved, just like suspicious Lola had said?

A chill skittered down her spine as she slumped against the side of the truck, peering past the side mirror, into the back of the cabin. Sure enough, it was packed full with black plastic trash bags. Step by step, she crept to the back of the truck. The bed had been piled high with them, too.

They knew they'd been found, and were cleaning out the meth shed, getting rid of the evidence.

At that moment, something up ahead in the darkness caught her eye. Not far ahead, only about a hundred yards or so, but partially hidden by a thick curtain of branches and leaves.

A dull but ever-brightening light, glowing like a rising sun on the edge of the horizon.

She sucked in a breath as she realized, with a start, where the light was coming from. The shed. The light was now spreading, infecting the darkness around it, orange and bright and wild.

Fire.

Warren and Tina . . . they were burning it all down. Erasing every trace of their wrongdoing. Leaving everything in ruins, the way that Sam and Tina had left Long Lakes, months ago.

And Jack . . . where was he?

A harrowing thought hit her like a bolt of lightning, shocking her to her very core.

Quickly tying Sunny's reins to a tree, Valentina skirted around the truck and broke into a feverish run, toward the growing inferno.

Chapter Twenty-Seven

This is bad.

Around him, the flames licked the walls, climbing ever higher as Jack willed his legs to move.

Of all the thoughts cycling through the tornado of his mind, only one seemed to come to the front of it. Lily and Brayden.

The image in his mind was of one of the nicest days he could remember. They'd gone on a vacation to Myrtle Beach when Lily was four and Brayden, not even two. Yvonne had been complaining that he'd been burning the midnight oil with work, and so he'd torn himself away for that one week. It'd been nice. Watching them squealing in glee as they chased the waves down the beach, lying in the sun for hours with the tight feeling of salt water baking into their skin, and then having cocktails on the back porch, in front of a shamelessly garish tropical sunset, after the kids were in bed. They'd made love almost every night, that trip, and he'd made a promise to make things up to her. On the drive back, holding hands, he told her they'd make that trip a yearly tradition.

But then he'd gotten too busy with work, and they'd never gone back.

Dammit.

He knew things were over with Yvonne. He didn't miss her as much as he expected to. She'd found someone who was much more her soul mate than he could ever be. But he'd always thought he still had time to repair his relationship with his kids. But now, that time had run out.

No.

With revived purpose, he looked around, gauging his situation.

The smoke was getting thicker and blacker, and he began to choke for the first time. His vision bled, all the bright colors reminding him of that Myrtle Beach sunset. Tears veiled his eyes. The intense heat seared his skin as he took the collar of his flannel shirt, pulling it up. He stretched it over his nose and mouth then put his blood-sticky palms down flat on the dirt. Using every last bit of strength he had left, he dragged both legs in, pushed his back against the wall, and slid his upper half up against it, the fabric of his flannel snagging on splinters in the wood, until the top of his head smashed against the windowsill.

By then he could no longer feel pain. His mind had blocked it out, perhaps. Grabbing onto the protruding part of the window frame for dear life, he twisted himself around to the wall and bore all his weight on it, feeling the cool glass of the window panes on his fingertips. Meanwhile, flames crackled behind him, coming ever closer. His head pounded, the dizziness and gravity threatening to drag him back down as the air in the cabin became increasingly toxic.

Eyes watering, he felt the edge of the window for a pull, a crank, a lock, anything to tell him that the window could be opened. Finding nothing, he let out a growl of exasperation. Still bracing himself against the windowsill, he jabbed his elbow against the glass of the pane. Once, twice . . . on the third time, it shattered.

He pushed against it again to clear away the glass, then dipped his head down to suck in the fresh air. Smoke billowed around him, fighting him to escape out in the night. The pane itself was too small, he couldn't even slip his head through.

Through the darkness and the haze, the thought he saw a form, running towards him. But then he blinked again, and it was gone.

All his energy expended, he felt his legs wobbling, giving out on him. He held onto the windowsill until the very last second, dragging as much fresh air into his lungs as he possibly could, before the blackness consumed him.

Beyond the sharp whip-snapping of flames behind him, he heard another loud crack, and the creak of a door opening.

He thought he heard someone calling his name, in a frantic, high-pitched voice. But it sounded faraway, as if at the end of a long tunnel. If it was help, he thought for sure it'd never reach him in time. He'd done all he could, and this was the end.

Lily, Brayden . . . he thought.

"Jack!"

Closer now. Valentina.

Two thoughts gripped him, almost simultaneously. First, a sense of relief, followed right afterwards by *Why is she here? Doesn't she know she's going to get herself killed? We're both going to die in here, because of me.*

Eyes useless, his hands groped through the darkness, seeking her out, but they grabbed at nothing but air.

Losing his grip on the edge of the window, he slipped into the billowing black clouds that threatened to smother him.

The second he hit the ground, warm, soft fingers laced with his.

At first, he thought it was a dream, or an angel, come to whisk him off to whatever came after this life. But when the hand in his yanked him with a sharp cry and pain screamed up to his injured shoulder, he realized it was Valentina.

She was still fighting, and she seemed far from giving up. She wouldn't leave him to die, alone. He had to fight, too, or else kill both of them.

That left no other option.

Somehow, he managed to climb to his feet, using all of her remarkable strength to right himself. She wrapped her arm around him and dragged him, limping and sagging on her slim frame, to the door, through a wall of midnight black smoke. He'd lost most of his vision and didn't know up from down, but Valentina knew. She guided him without hesitation, back through the doorway.

They exploded out into the night, choking and gasping, the air cold on their skin. She pulled him a safe distance from the burning cabin before she slowed to a stop, wavering on her feet. The second she loosened her grip, even a little, he fell to his knees. The familiar pain in his shoulder came screaming back, but he was alive. Miraculously. Barely. She fell beside him, coughing.

Still half-blind, lying on his side, he looked over at her, astonished. All he could make out in the darkness and smoke was her outline, silhouetted in the orange light of the fire, but at that moment, his heart swelled. She'd done this for him.

She crawled closer, concern lacing her voice. "Are you all right? I was so worried!"

Skin black with the smoke, hair covered in ash and bits of leaves, this woman—this crazy, incredible, strong woman—had done something no one had ever done before. She'd saved him.

He opened up his mouth to say something to her, words of appreciation and love, but his throat felt like he'd swallowed razor blades. All he could let out was a low groan.

Blue police lights shone in the distance, and everything came back. Warren. Tina. The drug house. The nightmare that had been these past few hours.

It only occurred to him that the danger could still be out there when he heard the crunching of branches nearby, away from the burning cabin. Everything else seemed so remarkably still, so peaceful, and yet, those people had tried to kill him before, and they'd do it again.

He cleared his throat to tell her that this wasn't safe, that they should get away, run, hide from this place, as soon as possible.

Before he could, he heard the unmistakable sound of a gun being cocked.

He blinked hard, frantic.

And when his vision cleared, he saw Warren Harvey, holding a very stiff and frightened Valentina, her back against his chest, and the barrel of a gun flush against her temple.

Chapter Twenty-Eight

Valentina dare not move.

She dare not flinch.

With the cold barrel of the gun pressed against her temple, she dare not even breathe.

She'd heard that before, that in moments of trauma, one's life flashes before her eyes. She never knew how true it was. She thought of her home in Milan, and of Antonio, on her wedding day, and how happy and young and innocent she was, expecting that happily ever after. She thought of Bea, who she hadn't seen in weeks, who'd now be alone in the States. And she thought of Jack, and how he'd brought her out of the deepest, darkest time of her life, into the light.

Was it all over now? Was she going to die because of this, because she'd attempted to save the man she loved? He'd lied to her, yes, but she knew he hadn't done it to be malicious or deceitful. He'd done it to protect her.

And she'd never *told* him she loved him. Would it go unsaid, forever?

Warren gripped her hard across the chest, pulling her back against his broad frame, stirring her from these maudlin thoughts to the present. He smelled like gasoline and sweat as he yanked her backwards, his tight hold pulling on her hair. Her feet slipped on the wet leaves on the gravel as she did her best to resist.

But there was no resisting. Warren was a big man, far too strong, and far too determined to get what he wanted. "What do you want from me?" she whispered.

"Shut up," he growled.

The lights of the roaring fire illuminated Jack's face. He'd once looked beaten and exhausted, but now his eyes were sharp and acutely tuned to the situation in front of him. "Let her go," he said, his voice calm and even.

"Hell if I will," Warren grunted, driving the gun even harder against the side of her head, making her desperately aware that with one simple pull, one tiny motion, it would all be over.

Jack took one small step toward the two of them, but Warren tightened his grip on Valentina, his big forearm sliding up to her throat and nearly crushing her windpipe. She threw her hands around his arm, trying to pry herself free, to gasp for air, but he didn't move.

"Take one step closer and I'll kill her."

Jack raised his bound hands carefully. "Take it easy," he said in a calm voice. "What do you want?"

He motioned into the darkness, where Valentina could see Sunny, hovering at the edge of the forest, nervously stamping her feet and bobbing her head. He leaned into her ear and said, "See that horse of yours? You and I are going to take a little ride. Then, when we get to your truck, you're going to give me the keys. And then it's no business of yours, what I do. Got it?"

Eyes on Jack, Valentina was only half-listening. He seemed to be trying to communicate something to her, but she wasn't sure what. All she knew was that if she went with Warren, she might never see Jack again. *And then I'll never be able to tell him I love him. Why had I never said it before?*

"Come on, Warren. Give it up. It's over," Jack shouted, his voice so loud, it echoed through the forest. She knew what he was doing, trying draw the police out of the woods. But were they even out there anymore? Maybe he'd killed them, too. And where was Tina?

One thing was sure. Warren Harvey was a desperate man, and there was no telling what he might do out of sheer desperation. He'd already proven he was willing to stop at nothing.

So when he pulled her toward the horse, she had no choice but to go along with it, dragging her feet slowly, hoping for a miracle.

Jack looked up, down, and around, for some way to get her out of this. She could almost see the gears in his head turning. But there was nothing to be done. If she didn't go with Warren, someone else would likely wind up dead. "All right, let's go."

"Drop your weapon!" a voice shouted.

Warren swung Valentina violently to the side to face the newest opponent, one of the police officers, emerging from the forest, gun drawn.

He laughed, but his laugh was through clenched teeth. "Sorry, boys. I think I have a better option. Stay back unless you want her dead."

On Jack's other side, another police officer emerged, his weapon poised to shoot. Tension crackled in the air, like the flames piercing the night sky.

A wild thought occurred to her. She could make a run for it. Head for the woods, and hope the police officers shot first. But there was always a chance that the officers would hesitate, and Warren was beyond hesitation, now. She'd get a bullet in her back. If it had been *Jack* holding the gun, it'd be a different story. She trusted Jack.

Right now, her heart thudding beneath her chest wall, she was too scared to do anything but what Warren wanted.

Behind them, the fire continued to rage, throwing off white embers that drifted down like bright snowflakes. He motioned to the horse and whispered into her ear, "Grab the reins."

She did as she was told, grasping the leather in one hand and leading Sunny close to her. She patted her warm side, feeling her pulse beating underneath her trim coat. The horse was scared to death and was stomping and frantically pulling at her reins. "It's all right," she whispered, partly to Sunny, and partly to herself.

"Get on."

Taking hold of the horn of the saddle, she put a foot in the stirrup and hoisted herself up.

No sooner had she thrown her leg over than a voice screamed out, loud, from the darkness. "Warren!"

Tina. She was rushing for them, covered in dirt, her head bleeding, dried leaves in her blonde ponytail. Her eyes were wild.

All heads swung in her direction but one.

Before Warren knew what was happening, Jack had lunged, hitting him square in the stomach, groping for his gun. Warren let out a guttural groan as the two went flying back to the ground, locked in a struggle, the gun caught somewhere between their bodies as each one fought for control.

Valentina gasped. "Jack!" Underneath her, Sunny whinnied. Nearby, the police stood, guns pointed, unsure of what to do. Tina screamed.

In the midst of all the chaos, a single gunshot rang out, so loud it rattled Valentina's eardrums.

And then, absolute stillness. Absolute silence. Even the wind and the fire seemed to quiet. It was like the whole forest was holding its collective breath.

Chapter Twenty-Nine

Before he even opened his eyes, Jack knew he wasn't in his own bed. It was the whirring and beeping of machinery around him that tipped him off, the scratch of the sheets on his skin, the harness of the mattress underneath him . . . all of these things tipped him off.

Not to mention, the pain. He felt like he'd gone fifteen rounds in a heavyweight fight. Everything hurt.

But in the first moments of wakefulness, as bright light danced beyond his closed eyelids, he couldn't remember a single thing that had brought him to this place. He thought of Brayden and Lily, and of that night, on the quiet dock with Valentina, feeling, for the first time in his life, completely content with his place in the world. And then . . . nothing.

Slowly, it came back to him. The frantic ride on horseback, the pain shattering through his body as he fell from the horse. The cabin afire, the flames nearly searing his skin. The confrontation with Warren, who'd been holding a gun to Valentina's head. And then . . .

And then . . .

Hell, he couldn't remember. But Valentina had been in danger.

His eyes snapped open, his vision bleary in the jarring fluorescent light. He blinked a few times, trying to regain his vision, and rasped, his throat sandpaper-dry, "Valentina?"

Instead, it was a man in khakis and a plaid shirt who came wandering into his vision, standing at the foot of his bed. When the man peered closer, Jack's vision finally cooperated. It was Louie Valdez, from his office.

He smacked Jack on the foot. "Hey. You're up. How're you doing?"

Jack looked around. Aside from Louie, the room was empty. Stark, as hospital rooms usually were, though the pale peach walls and paintings of woodland scenes on the walls tried to convey otherwise. The machinery and hospital equipment around the room easily overpowered any attempts at hominess. But Jack wasn't interested in any of that. Had he left Valentina in the clutches of that asshole? Passed out and let him get away?

Shit. He couldn't remember.

"Where's Valentina?" he croaked, ignoring the question.

"Relax," Louie said. "You're in Cookeville hospital. You're going to be fine. You got yourself in a little mess, didn't you? Erica . . . shit."

He closed his eyes, remembering the last time he'd spoken with her. "She's dead, isn't she?"

He nodded. "Yeah. But they apprehended the people responsible. Turned out that developer you were looking into was in some real shady shit, and bankruptcy fraud was only the tip of the iceberg. We got him, his wife, a couple of the dealers who worked with him and lived in the neighborhood . . ."

"And Warren? What happened to him?"

"Don't you remember? Dead. You shot him." When Jack shook his head, Louie continued. "Bank president was actually the ringleader. We think he killed his wife, too, a few months back. They've been running this operation for a while. Been supplying most of the county with meth. Let me tell you, you're back in Dees' good graces. He's *thrilled*. I think you're gunning for a promotion, man."

It was a relief, but it wasn't an answer to the original question. Jack stared, waiting for more. "All right. But what about Valentina?"

"She's the woman who came in with you, right?" he asked. "She's fine. Out in the waiting room. You're in critical condition. They're limiting visitors."

He let out a sigh of relief. "Can I see her?"

Louie nodded and reached into his backpack. "I'll ask," he said, lifting out his phone. "I'm going to call Yvonne. She's worried about you. She didn't tell Brayden, but Lily is worried about you. She was in the car when Yvonne got the call, so she heard everything. She made you this."

He handed Jack a hand-drawn card that had a big red heart on it, then left, sweeping his phone up to his ear. Jack's heart tugged in a thousand different directions as he read the words: *I love you, Daddy.*

Opening the card, tears pricked at the corners of his eyes as he read:

Dear Daddy. Please be okay. Bray and I love you so so so so so much and want you to feel better soon. I miss you.

Love, Lily

There was a stick figure of two people hugging inside. He stared at the picture, running his finger over the crayon artwork, knowing that Lily had touched this same paper. He imagined her lying on her stomach on her bed, her brow furrowed like it always did when she was concentrating really hard on something, pouring all her love into this card. He smiled.

"Is that from your children?" as voice at the door said.

He looked up to see Valentina, standing in the doorway. Her eyes looked red-rimmed from crying and worry, and she wore no make-up, but she looked as beautiful as ever.

He nodded and showed it to her. "Lily is my oldest. She drew this for me."

Valentina came to his bedside and smiled. "It's very nice. Bea was worried for me, too. She came out this morning from college and is out in the waiting room, with Michelle. It was so nice to see her. I was too much of a wreck to be here by myself."

"Are you okay?" he asked her.

She laughed. "How can you ask me that? *You* are the one in the hospital. I am fine. How are you?"

For the first time, he noticed the massive bandage on his shoulder. "Been better."

"Can I get you anything?"

He motioned to the water. She went and took two glasses, pouring one for him, and one for herself. She handed it to him. "I know. My throat has been so dry, ever since the fire."

His lungs still ached from the smoke, and really, every last bit of him felt like it had something wrong with it. But when Valentina settled next to him and took his hand, it felt like everything was on the mend. He held up the glass in his free hand. "Uh, it's not wine, but . . . What should we toast to?"

She laughed. At least he could make her smile, even after everything that they'd been through. It did feel like they'd known each other for ages, but that's what traumatic situations often did—as much as they could rend people apart, they also had a way of thrusting people together. But now that it was all over, what happened next was up to them.

And more than anything, he wanted this to continue.

"So you know the truth? That I'm not a writer?"

She nodded.

"And you're not angry?"

"No. Ordinarily, I'd hate it. I hate lies. But I understand why you couldn't tell me. You had a good reason. You were undercover."

"Yes. I tried to tell you the truth as much as possible. The last thing I wanted to do was lie to you, Valentina."

She leaned in and kissed his forehead gently. "The way I see it, maybe it *will* be true. I think you could write a book about this, one day, if you want. And I can help. In the future."

He liked the sound of that. "Maybe I could."

"And I think that in the future, while you're recovering, you should spend some time in Long Lakes. Maybe at *Elsewhere*, this time?"

"Elsewhere," he murmured. He liked the sound of that, even more. He looked down at the glass in his hand. "So I think that's what we toast to. *Elsewhere.*"

She smiled and lifted her glass. "To *Elsewhere.*"

They clinked glasses. He took a long gulp, and while she took a dainty sip of her own, he stroked her hand. Right then, all the past's mistakes seemed so far away, they didn't matter. What mattered was ahead. Maybe soon, he'd write of his experiences, or maybe he'd simply use the time given to him to enjoy the people he loved, as much and as fully as possible.

And *Elsewhere* looked very enticing indeed.

THE END

Made in the USA
Monee, IL
09 April 2022

94475085R00144